COORDINATING THE CRIMINAL JUSTICE SYSTEM

A Guide to Improve the Effective Administration of Justice

Leslie J. Smith

University Press of America,® Inc.
Lanham · Boulder · New York · Toronto · Plymouth, UK

Copyright © 2008 by
University Press of America®, Inc.
4501 Forbes Boulevard
Suite 200
Lanham, Maryland 20706
UPA Acquisitions Department (301) 459-3366

Estover Road
Plymouth PL6 7PY
United Kingdom

Library of Congress Control Number: 2007937974
ISBN-13: 978-0-7618-3939-2 (paperback : alk. paper)
ISBN-10: 0-7618-3939-9 (paperback : alk. paper)

⊖™ The paper used in this publication meets the minimum
requirements of American National Standard for Information
Sciences—Permanence of Paper for Printed Library Materials,
ANSI Z39.48—1984

For Lisa and our son Brent

Contents

Figures

Preface

As a criminal justice coordinator and university instructor, I was compelled to write this criminal justice guide because of the lack of literature addressing the coordination of U.S. criminal justice systems. I was also concerned about not having a text that explained and consolidated the conceptual relationships between sociology and criminal justice. It is important to move beyond merely seeing what is around us, and also notice the ways that enable us to understand society more systematically. The criminal justice system's organizational environment is social life, and therefore it is difficult to study the criminal justice system without addressing the sociological factors such as the cultural, ecological, economic, political, legal, technological, and demographic forces.

This guide addresses these issues by providing a step-by-step strategy that clarifies complex issues associated with coordinating the criminal justice system. As a resource, it is ideal for individuals who are not trained or considered experts in criminal justice and should encourage students, criminal justice planners and others to try their own hands-on approach to coordinating the criminal justice process. It may be of particular interest to individuals charged with the responsibility to coordinate their local criminal justice systems. Above all, as criminal justice presses forward to the future, this guide will assist in bridging the gap between traditional and contemporary approaches to criminal justice administration.

Because my original study, addressing the administration of state criminal justice systems (Appendix A) did not thoroughly address the administrative and planning components of this process; this book finalizes the study and is considered the *sequel.*

Leslie J. Smith
July 2007

Introduction

Since 2001, more that half a million people have departed from U.S. prisons and returned to neighborhoods across the country. This increase in the movement from prison to the community has come at a time when U.S. criminal justice systems are not performing at optimal levels. A study released by the U.S. Department of Justice in June 2002, entitled *Recidivism of Prisoners Released in 1994* revealed of the nearly 300,000 prisoners released in 15 states in 1994, 67 percent were rearrested within three years.

Much of the debate on the performance of the criminal justice system focuses on whether the system's coordination and planning processes are adequate, and if there is a need for a more unifying philosophy. The literature suggests that the criminal justice goals of retribution, deterrence, incapacitation, and rehabilitation are inordinately fragmented due to a preoccupation with the crime control mandate and the rejection of the basic purpose of the criminal justice system: a *corrections* system committed to punishment and rehabilitation with the goal of reducing recidivism. Because each agent of the criminal justice system has different mandates it is unlikely that this goal will be reached, hence, the reason for the current high recidivism rates. The political profit made from law and order platforms is also declining as states realize the disproportionate costs related to what many experts have identified as one-dimensional and ineffective criminal justice practices. Serious policy questions remain about the investment of any additional resources until a more balanced approach to criminal justice develops.

The Dallas County District Attorney's Office may be providing the balance that is needed. As revealed in an article which appeared in the *Fort Worth Star Telegram* on April 1, 2007, District Attorney Craig Watkins announced that the mission of the D.A.'s Office will focus more on *justice* than convictions. He articulated a vision that calls for strong punishment for hardened criminals but also includes room for diversion programs, intervention, and a community court system. Craig Watkins swept in on a Democratic tide in the 2007 election, along with more than 40 judges.

The key to addressing these issues is the establishment of a criminal justice planning process that requires performance to be measured in terms of achieving the goals and objectives of each component of the criminal justice system collectively. Although the legislative, judicial and executive branches of the U.S. government are constitutionally independent and not required to engage in any coordinated planning activities, these requirements should not lead to poor performance. It is essential to promote positive government through increased collaboration between governmental departments. The past 20 years have been characterized by increased coordination, cooperation, and improved approaches to criminal justice planning and this strategy must prevail. Since the inception of the criminal justice system, these bureaucratic factors have been challenging, but they have been overcome by criminal justice organizations that have demonstrated good ideas, good *leadership*, and good communication.

STEP 1

VIEW THE CRIMINAL JUSTICE SYSTEM AS ONE ORGANIZATION

The scope, origins, mission and coordination of the criminal justice system are addressed in Steps 1-9. The issue is whether the justice system can be viewed as one organization and each component as a sub-unit. It is further argued whether the criminal justice system is a system, process, network, or non-system, and whether there is a need for a constructive program at every point in the system. It is emphasized how each element of the criminal justice system must work collectively in order to impact the total system outcomes and how a decrease in recidivism is identified as the measures of success.

As previously indicated, by design, U.S. criminal justice systems attempt to decrease criminal behavior through a variety of separated and uncoordinated processes, and each system component is not required to engage in any coordinated planning effort. However, for the student of criminal justice or a future criminal justice planner, it is suggested that you view the criminal justice system as one organization and each component as a sub-unit. Units within the criminal justice system have their own performance measures: arrest rates for police, conviction levels for prosecutors, appeals for courts, and numbers of escapes, infractions and riots for correctional agencies. In recent years, the criminal justice system began to accept that performance should be measured in terms of achieving the goals and objectives of each component of the criminal justice system collectively. While it is consistent with the traditional focus on the process of criminal justice to emphasize process measures, it is important to find new ways to improve our understanding of the measurement of the subunits and the entire system in achieving the objectives of the criminal justice system. If this more monolithic concept is utilized properly, justice administrators (i.e., police, prosecution, courts, and corrections officials) will have the opportunity to provide more leadership over a system in order to accomplish its mission to reduce and control crime. It will also neutralize the argument that U.S. criminal justice

systems attempt to decrease criminal behavior through a wide variety of uncoordinated and sometimes uncomplimentary efforts and that each component system fails to engage in any coordinated planning effort; hence, the components
are often characterized by friction, conflict and miscommunication (Peak 2004).

Crime rates and recidivism have long served as critical measures for the
performance of the nation's criminal justice system. However, it is important for
you to understand that the community and the promotion of non-criminal justice
options should also be included as performance indicators. These measures represent the basic goals of public safety to which all components of the criminal
justice system contribute (U.S. Department of Justice 1993). As Peters and
Waterman, authors of *In Search of Excellence*, put it: "Figure out what your
value system is. Decide what your company stands for" (1982, pp.227). The
same principle applies to social and nonprofit organizations. Before a criminal
justice agency can evaluate their performance, they must first define their mission and what they are attempting to achieve.

Professor Charles H. Logan of the University of Connecticut describes the
major purposes (i.e., mission) of the criminal justice system in terms of four
civic ideals (U.S. Department of Justice 1993):

1.   Doing justice
2.   Promoting secure communities
3.   Restoring crime victims
4.   Promoting non-criminal options (i.e., social/community justice) [1]

He explains that justice can be defined as the quality of treating individuals
according to their civic rights and in ways that they deserve to be treated by virtue of relevant conduct. Criminal justice is rights-respecting treatment that is
deserved by virtue of criminal conduct as judged by the rule of law. Thus, *doing
justice* implies at least four things: hold offenders fully accountable for their
offenses, protect offenders' constitutional and legal rights, treat like offenses
alike, and take into account relevant differences among offenders and offenses.
Therefore, the literature suggests that the criminal justice system may be viewed
as a single entity with *justice* as the primary mission followed by community
safety, victim services, and social justice, and each sub-unit of the system as a
vehicle to achieve these goals. Therefore, in order to meet the justice goal, it is
suggested to link the mission of the criminal justice system to each of the system's components. In turn, each criminal justice department must coordinate the
development of individual mission statements for their departments in conjunction with the mission of the criminal justice system, and identify their performance goals and objectives accordingly. For example:

Mission of Criminal Justice System [2]

To jointly strive to enforce lawful standards of conduct; protect individuals and communities; and become more community-based; assist victims; improve institutional capabilities; and engage the community and its citizens in crime prevention while preserving individual civil liberties and protecting basic human rights.

Mission of Police Agency

The police agency should work to minimize the reliance on traditional law enforcement practices; become more community-based; decentralize operations; and must comprehensively address community safety, crime prevention, and human rights in the performance of their duties.

Performance Goal

The police agency will decentralize the existing Operations Division of the police department and establish a community-based policing program.

Performance Objectives

Officers within the Operations Division will begin:

1) Training in community-based policing (COP).
2) Acquiring building space and other accommodations to support COP.
3) Survey the community that will be impacted by the COP services.

Another example may be found within a county based strategic plan titled *Tarrant County Strategic Plan* (Lyle Sumek Associates, Inc. 2002, pp. 10). This plan delineates the need to provide a countywide vision, mission, and goals statement. It suggests that the vision be integrated into the key elements of the comprehensive strategic plan; into policies, projects, and plans; into decisions and actions and into daily operations; the mission defines the business of county government and must be incorporated into each county department. It explains that mission and goals assist each department in the development of core services, programs, and products; provides meaning to citizens and employees; and establishes performance measures and a continuous improvement process for evaluating performance, organization process, and exploring new and more innovate and cost-effective ways for providing and implementing services.

The criminal justice goal for this plan is defined as the need to have a safe county for its people, with the objectives addressing improvements in emergency management and response times, coordination with area law enforcement agencies, working relationships with courts and corrections, more effective criminal justice information systems, and the timely processing of cases in the court system. If you were interested in introducing new goals and objectives in this plan such as a new justice model addressing reintegration as the goal, it must be incorporated into the strategic plan and considered a new planning objective, which will be coordinated with the community, law enforcement, prosecutor, and courts and corrections at the local and state level.

Sociology Reference:

Sociological references are used throughout this guide. Although not comprehensive, these references will provide the reader with the general understanding of the social, legal, political, economic, demographic, and cultural forces surrounding the criminal justice system. The references are placed after a Step with which there is a relationship, but they may also be duplicated throughout the guide. Except where otherwise indicated, the sociological references were obtained from The Blackwell Dictionary of Sociology, 2nd edition, Blackwell Publishers, Inc., by Allan G. Johnson (2005).

Social System: A social system is any interdependent set of cultural and structural elements that can be thought of as a unit. The parts of a social system can be of almost any size or complexity and may include a word, friend, department stores, corporations, and *governments*. In general, any system can be defined as a set of mutually supporting elements or parts that can be thought of as a whole (i.e., a motor, the human body as a system, or a criminal justice system)

Works Cited

Peters, T.J. and R.H. Waterman Jr., 1982. *In Search of Excellence.* New York, New York, Harper Collins.

Peak, Kenneth J. 2004. *Justice Administration*, pp.6-15.Upper Saddle River, New Jersey: Pearson Prentice Hall.

Smith, L. J. 2003. "The Organizational Environment and its Influence on State Criminal Justice Systems within the U.S. and the Offender Reintegration Process" *Criminal justice Studies.* 16(2): pp. 97-112.

Sumek, L. 2002. *Tarrant County, Texas. Strategic Plan 2002-2006. Commissioners Court.* pp. 10. Lyle Sumek Associates, Inc.

U.S. Department of Justice, Bureau of Justice Statistics, *Performance Measures for the Criminal Justice System* October 1993. (NCJ-143505).

Notes

1. These four variables are suggested as measurable variables within a multi-dimensional performance model that evaluates crime rates, recidivism rates, performance measures of a justice institution's programs and practices, community performance measures, and victimization. (refer to the U.S. Department of Justice, Bureau of Justice Statistics, *Performance Measures for the Criminal Justice System,* October 1993, NCJ-143505. **http://www.ojp.usdoj.gov/bjs/pub/pdf/pmcjs.pdf**

2. The mission statement delineated in this example is intentionally structured to change the traditional mission of a criminal justice organization. The traditional criminal justice model is structured with less community involvement.

STEP 2

HAVE A COMPLETE UNDERSTANDING OF THE ORIGINS OF THE CRIMINAL JUSTICE SYSTEM

It is necessary for you to have a complete understanding of the origins of the criminal justice system before you can attempt to change it. The original concept of criminal justice was introduced in 1967 by the Commission on Law Enforcement and Administration of Justice in the report titled *The Challenge of Crime in a Free Society*. The use of the "flow chart" was included in the report titled "A General View of the Criminal Justice System." [1] This same flow chart has been reproduced numerous times in criminal justice textbooks throughout the years. This graphic conveys the scope of the crime at various stages in crime processing by delineating the process and interrelationship of police, prosecution, courts, and corrections. This more *systematic approach* to evaluating the criminal justice system was intended to improve the effectiveness, of the criminal justice system and as a result of this effort it is now considered a planning model and a focus of study in criminal justice administration.

In June of 1997, the U.S. Department of Justice held a symposium to celebrate and commemorate the 30th Anniversary of the 1967 President's Crime Commission. Members and staff from the 1967 Commission were invited to share their experiences with criminal justice professionals in the field today. The symposium served as a reminder of the progress that has been made in achieving the goals set forth by the President's Commission on Law Enforcement and Administration of Justice towards establishing a more systematic approach to criminal justice. The symposium delineated that as a result of this initiative criminal justice has become a discipline, and has taken greater steps toward professionalism (U.S. Department of Justice 1998). Charles F. Wellford from the University of Maryland, a symposium panelist, is author of the report titled "Changing Nature of Criminal Justice System Responses and Its Professions." Wellford explained that the flow chart embodied one of the central themes of the Commission's analysis of justice in our society: the need to create better understanding of the criminal justice system *qua* system, and a better understanding of the ways in which actions taken at any point in the system can affect other ele-

ments of the system. The chart outlined the interrelationship of police, prosecution, courts, and corrections for the *first time.* The chart created a better understanding of "cause and effect" and systemic thinking, was the central theme of
the Commission and was portrayed as the first step in identifying the components of the criminal justice system that could be manipulated to determine their
effect on the remainder of the system. This process was identified as the meth-
odology of system analysis (pp.58-62). [2]

Sociology Reference:

Social Control: A concept that refers to the ways in which people's
thoughts, feelings, appearance, and behavior are regulated in social systems. To
some degree control is exerted through various forms of coercion, from the par-
ent's ability to physically restrain a child to the *authority of criminal justice systems* to imprison those convicted of crimes and the authority of physicians to
administer drugs that make difficult patients more manageable.

Works Cited

U. S. Department of Justice, *The Challenge of Crime in a Free Society: Looking
Back Looking Forward,* pp.1-78. February 1998.
http://www.ojp.usdoj.gov/reports/98Guides/lblf/lblf.txt (accessed June 2, 2007)

Notes

1.   The reader can reference the "flow chart" at **www.ojp.usdoj.gov/bjs** /
or send comments to **askbjs@usdoj.gov**.

2.   There are efforts to develop system-wide performance models. The
1970's JUSSIM model is a system-wide performance model. It is an interactive
computer program for which an accompanying data file describes the flow diagram of a criminal justice system, the branching ratios of the flow between
stages, the resources consumed, and the costs and workloads. This model was
implemented to help develop a plan for a local criminal justice planning agency.
Source: *Journal of Research in Crime and Delinquency,* Vol. 10, No. 2, 117-131
(1973) DOI: 10.1177/002242787301000203 SAGE Publications. Refer to the
recent version of JUSSIM 1995 released by the State of Kentucky.

STEP 3

BECOME FAMILIAR WITH EACH COMPONENT OF THE CRIMINAL JUSTICE SYSTEM AND USE IT AS A FRAME OF REFERENCE

It is important for you to understand how each component of the criminal justice system functions in order to develop a frame of reference. The Bureau of Justice Statistics Criminal Justice Flow Chart provides a step-by-step description of each component of the criminal justice process. You can reference the "flow chart" at the U.S. Department of Justice Bureau of Justice Statistics (BJS) Web page at **www.ojp.usdoj.gov./bjs**. The information below is a general overview of the unidirectional processes associated with the U.S. criminal justice system as provided by the U. S. Department of Justice, Bureau of Justice Statistics:

Figure1: The flow of events in the U.S. Criminal Justice System integrated into a matrix format for clarification.

1. Police	-Enforce laws -Investigate crimes -Search people, vicinities, buildings -Arrest or detain people
2. Prosecution	-File charges -Seek indictments -Drop cases -Reduce charges
3. Courts	-Set bail or conditions for release

3. Courts	-Dismiss charges -Impose sentence -Revoke probation
4. Corrections	-Assign to type of correctional facility -Award privileges -Punish for disciplinary infractions
5. Parole	-Prisoner may become eligible for parole after serving a specific part of his or her sentence. Parole is the conditional release of a prisoner before the prisoner's full sentence has been served.

Source: U.S. Department of Justice, Bureau of Justice Statistics

In order to develop a planning model and to establish a frame of reference, utilize the flow chart as an *"as is to be"* model and compare past and present issues associated with the criminal justice system. Charles Wellford addressed the following points as they relate to present and past issues of the criminal justice system and may be used when attempting to structure a frame of reference (U.S. Department of Justice 1998).

• The original description of the criminal justice system was presented with case flow unidirectional (i.e., one-dimensional), and therefore was problematic.
• Previously, there was a preoccupation with system processes and subsystem outcomes.
• It is now important to pay equal attention total system outcomes.
• Changes at any point in the system can influence not only those activities that occur later in the system, but also the activities prior to that point of change. This has been a consistent issue from the inception of the criminal justice system.
• The original concept encouraged many to describe the criminal justice system
• It is now important to describe and assess the system.
• There is not enough emphasis on the impact of external influences (i.e., the organizational environment) of the criminal justice system. This has been a consistent issue from the inception of the criminal justice system.
• It is now important to identify the goals of our justice systems, describe in detail the processes used in those systems, and develop measures of both.
• It is important to continue to encourage the development of higher education and suggest criminal justice as the major field of study.
• The past 20 years have been characterized by increased coordination,

cooperation, and improved approaches to conducting research.

•   Since the inception of the criminal justice system, bureaucratic factors have been challenging, but they can be overcome within criminal justice organizations that demonstrate good ideas, good leadership, and good communication.

Wellford suggested that the Commission's work also helped us to understand, through its notion of a criminal justice system, the importance of collecting data at all of these points, and of recognizing the value of those data for different estimates and for understanding global indicators of the effectiveness of the system. It identified the need to collect data at all points in the system, both internal and external, and to address research, statistics, and data collection which changed all future approaches to conducting criminal justice research and planning. He explained that when agencies come together to solve a problem rather than implement a philosophy, coordination and cooperation occur. He clarified that it was the view of the Commission that there had to be a priority, and the first priority was *justice* and that crime control had to be achieved in the context of a free society (i.e., crime control through due process). In support of the Commission, Wellford explains that we need a system that is just, we want a system that reduces crime, or at least the harm associated with crime, and respects victims. We want a system that is safe for the people that work in the system and are affected by it. Wellford suggests that if there is one basis on which one can criticize the Commission's analysis of the criminal justice system, it is its emphasis on the effectiveness of the system in reducing crime and the relative absence of consideration of *how crime reduction could be achieved while ensuring justice* (U.S. Department of Justice 1998).

The Commission's work and the work of other contemporary criminal justice professionals provides the direction to finally achieve the goals the Commission established thirty-seven years ago. Although slowly developing, progress is being made. Leadership is the key. Current and future criminal justice leaders must continue to emphasize the need to learn and understand the Commission's "concept of criminal justice" in order to continue this effort. Although we remain years away from this goal, effective coordination, advancements in higher education, exceptional leadership, quality research, and improvement in technology will expedite this process, and a "systems analysis" approach will no longer be considered a concept but a sense of duty of our criminal justice leadership.

The following is an excerpt from the report titled *The Challenge of Crime in a Free Society: A Report by The President's Commission on Law Enforcement and Administration of Justice, February 1967.* This passage, written 37 years ago, ironically describes the state of present day U.S. criminal justice systems and suggests the same needs associated with improved coordination, professionalism, research, and technology.

"In sum, America's system of criminal justice is overcrowded and over-worked, undermanned, underfinanced, and very often misunderstood. It needs more information and more knowledge. It needs more *technical resources*. It needs more *coordination* among its many parts. It needs more public support. It needs the help of *community* programs and institutions in dealing with offenders and potential offenders. It needs, above all, the willingness to reexamine old ways of doing things, to reform itself, to experiment, to run risks, to date. It needs vision."

Sociology Reference:

Justice: A concept referring to fairness and to the process of people getting what they deserve. In a legal sense, justice consists of treating everyone according to the law, of guaranteeing civil rights and following prescribed procedures in a consistent manner.

Works Cited

U. S. Department of Justice, *The Challenge of Crime in a Free Society: Looking Back Looking Forward,* pp. 1-78 February 1998.

STEP 4

A COORDINATED APPROACH TO DEVELOP MISSION STATEMENTS

After you reach an agreement that the criminal justice system should be viewed as one organization and functions as a system, there must be a coordinated approach to develop formal mission and goal statements. A system as defined by Wikipedia (en.wikipedia.org/wiki/System) is an assemblage of interrelated elements comprising a unified whole. From the Latin and Greek, the term "system" meant to combine, to set up, to place together. A sub-system is a system that is part of another system. A system typically consists of components (or elements) that are connected together in order to facilitate the flow of information, matter, or energy.

It can be argued that the criminal justice system meets the above criteria for a system but functions very poorly; it attempts to decrease criminal behavior through a variety of uncoordinated processes; each system component fails to engage in any coordinated planning effort; these components are characterized by *broad discretion* resulting in systemic fragmentation, primarily conflict and poor communication (Peak 2005, pp. 6-7). As previously indicated, certain levels of systemic fragmentation of U.S. criminal justice systems are acceptable by intrinsic design. However, inordinate levels of fragmentation caused primarily by poor planning and coordination adversely impact the effective development of the organizational mission which, in turn, negatively impacts the relationship between criminal justice agencies, the effective development of a unifying criminal justice philosophy, and expected outcomes.

It is important to establish a commitment to collectively define the organizational mission for each component of the criminal justice system because it is the first step toward minimizing systemic fragmentation. Each person must be aware of the mission in order to establish effective policy making strategies. The following is an example of mission statements for each component of the criminal justice system, accompanied by its goals, objectives, and expected outcomes.

Mission of the Criminal Justice System

To seek justice, to jointly strive to enforce lawful standards of conduct; to protect individuals and promote secure communities; to assist victims; to improve institutional capabilities; and to be engaged in community justice and crime prevention while preserving individual civil liberties and protecting basic human rights.

Goals of the Criminal Justice System

- Effective punishment
- Fairness in sentencing
- Incarceration of the chronic offender
- Commitment to rehabilitation
- Preventative research
- Educational enhancement
- Effective administration of justice
- Advancement in technology
- Community-based problem solving
- Alternative to punishments

Objectives/Activities

Programs addressing the community, police, prosecution, courts and corrections agencies, such as community policing and prosecution, reentry courts, intermediate sanctions, chronic offender institutions; adjudication partnerships, organization and administration, career development; leadership and planning strategies, justice administration, technology, personnel administration, financial management, reintegration, crime causation, environmental design, leadership, drug treatment.

Criminal Justice System: Sub-System Outputs

The number of:
Reported crimes to police, arrests, cases filed, deferred, accepted, dismissed, forwarded, and the number of pleas, trials and convictions.

Criminal Justice System: Sub System Program Outputs

The number of:

Community oriented police (COPS) programs and community justice programs such as community prosecution and court programs, college degree programs, organizational and leadership surveys conducted, environmental design programs produced, countywide criminal case filing systems implemented, justice employee career development programs and employee promotions, court administration and case processing programs, drug court programs, and offender reintegration work programs

Criminal Justice System: Total System Outcomes

The percent of:

Decrease in crime; decrease in incarceration rates; increase of pretrial diversions, decrease in drug addictions, increase in 4-year college degrees for justice personnel, increase in justice employee retention rates, increase in jobs for offenders, increase in high school graduations for offenders, decrease in cases per court and court dockets, increase from the time of arrest to trial, decrease in jail population, decrease in truancy; increase in school attendance, increase in employee performance increase in effective reintegration, decrease in recidivism and an overall improvement in community safety.

The following are examples of mission statements for each component of the criminal justice system, each of which should coincide with the mission of the criminal justice system:

Mission of Law Enforcement

The police agency should work to establish justice as the primary goal, balance the reliance on traditional law enforcement practices with community-based practices, decentralize operations, and comprehensively address community safety, crime prevention, victim services, and human rights in the performance of their duties.

Mission of Prosecution

The prosecutor must establish justice as the primary goal, and continue to strive for maximum efficiency in case processing; balance traditional practices with more community-based initiatives; decentralize operations; maintain workable relationships with the community and police; uphold the rights of the accused; and ensure fairness throughout the justice system

Mission of Courts
The judiciary must preserve its traditional values of impartiality, equal justice, individuality, and fairness and become more community based. Sentencing practices must remain devoted to the effective use of punishment, sentencing disparities must be minimized, and community-based correctional programs facilitated.

Mission of Corrections

Community Corrections: Maintain established goals to protect public interest and safety by supervising the individuals placed on community supervision by the judiciary; enforce the orders of the court; and provide services to meet the needs of the offender that are grounded in evidence based practices in order to assist in the rehabilitation and reintegration process as well as becoming law-abiding citizens.

Institutional Corrections: Maintain the custodial goals of security and discipline; effectively address offender reintegration; instill humane conditions and treatment of all inmates; encourage sensitivity to cultural and gender diversity; implement programs that improve the institutional capability of correctional institutions in order to ensure community safety, and enhance effective interaction among inmates, officers, and correctional managers.

As previously indicated, seeking justice is the mission of the criminal justice system and the key goal of each component of the system, therefore, justice must be viewed as legitimate before we can proceed to controlling and preventing crime. These aforementioned mission statements are structured with justice in mind but doing justice is difficult to achieve and in many cases falls short of this ideal. However, a formal mission statement with a commitment to justice establishes a social allegiance that will fill the void that currently exists in the United States criminal justice systems. Without justice there is little difference between criminal justice in the United States or what is found in other authoritarian countries. It seems that *fairness* is the fundamental test: We want to have fair laws and arrest, investigate, judge, and punish fairly, all of which requires quality decision-making.

Sociology Reference:

Formal Organization: A formal organization is a social system organized around specific goals and usually consisting of several interrelated groups or subsystems. Formal organizations are governed by clearly stated, rigidly enforced norms. Corporations, the Catholic Church, court systems, university administrations and military organizations all have properties of formal organizations.

Works Cited

Peak, Kenneth J. 2004. *Justice Administration*, pp.6-7.Upper Saddle River, New Jersey: Pearson Prentice Hall.

STEP 5

QUALITY DECISION MAKING AT EACH LEVEL OF THE SYSTEM

Although brief, this step may be considered the most significant to you because effective decision making at each level of the system can be considered quality control. When seeking justice through crime control and due process goals, the quality (i.e., professional ethics) of the decision making process rests with a model of crime control that recognizes and respects individual rights (Peak 2004 pp. 16). As previously delineated, the mission of the criminal justice system is to jointly strive to enforce lawful standards of conduct; protect individuals and communities; and become more community-based; assist victims; improve institutional capabilities; and engage the community and its citizens in crime prevention while preserving individual civil liberties and protecting basic human rights. It is not possible to address this mission effectively without justice as the primary goal and quality decision making at each level of the system. This type of an ethical approach to crime control would be considered rational because it requires a *constructive program* at *every point of the system* and insists on the protection of the innocent, while providing for the accountability of the offender. This approach emphasizes community safety, accountability, and competency development (Bazemore and Umbreit 1994a).

The central theme of the above mission statement is the same as the Commission's: doing justice. Doing justice requires upholding the rights of individuals and punishing those who violate the law that reflects American values and is presented in the U.S. Constitution (i.e., crime control through due process). A good comparison of the crime control and due process models is found in Herbert Packer's 1968 publication titled *The Limits of the Criminal Sanction,* "Two Models of the Criminal Process," Stanford University Press (pp. 149-173). Packer describes these two competing models of criminal justice as contrasting ways of viewing the goals of and procedure of the criminal justice system. The crime control model is more administrative, with repression of crime as the goal and the due process model is structured with the goal to preserve individual liberties. Although no criminal justice organization functions solely within one model or the other, the balance is a criminal justice strategy structured to include both models: crime control through due process.

Sociology Reference:

Justice: A concept referring to fairness and to the process of people getting what they deserve. In a legal sense, justice consists of treating everyone according to the law, of guaranteeing civil rights and following prescribed procedures in a consistent manner.

Works Cited

Basemore, G., and M. Umbreit (1994a). Rethinking the sanctioning function in juvenile court: Retributive or restorative responses to youth crime, Unpublished manuscript.

Peak, Kenneth J. 2004 *Justice Administration*, pp.6,7,16 Upper Saddle River, New Jersey: Pearson Prentice Hall.

STEP 6

ESTABLISH ORGANIZED AND COORDINATED PLANNING STRATEGIES

Criminal Justice Coordinating Committees

The U.S. Department of Justice, National Institute of Corrections (January 2002) introduced a more organized and coordinated planning strategy that minimizes systemic fragmentation. This strategy, considered a comprehensive approach to criminal justice planning, is titled *Guidelines for Developing a Criminal Justice Coordinating Committee.* This guide delineates the advantages of criminal justice planning partnerships, resulting in a better understanding of crime and criminal justice problems, greater communication and cooperation among agencies and units of local government, improved analysis of problems, clearer objectives and priorities, more effective resource allocation, and improved programs services and personnel. This NIC suggests that this type of a planning strategy increases public confidence and support for the criminal justice processes, thus enhancing system performance. Criminal Justice Coordinating Committee provides the *planning structure* necessary to coordinate and merge the mission goals and objectives of each component of the criminal justice system, thus enhancing the mission of the criminal justice system as a whole. It is suggested that you utilize the DOJ guide to develop a criminal justice coordinating committee in your jurisdiction. A coordinating committee of this type can be utilized at the *local, state, and national levels* and is considered one of the best planning strategies to improve the effective administration of justice.

Local and state criminal justice systems are constantly under pressure to plan more efficiently and effectively without diminishing the quality of their services. Problems associated with backlogged dockets, crowded jails, and recidivism is becoming commonplace. For example, changes in a county's jail population, especially in counties experiencing growth, can affect the demand for jail space. Collaborative efforts to address various criminal justice-related issues through criminal justice coordinating committees are becoming more important for mounting an efficient and effective response to these problems. The creation of planning partnerships of this type has emerged as one of the solutions to improve communication among criminal justice agencies in order to deal with these complex issues (U.S. Department of Justice 1999, pp. 1). A criminal justice coordinating committee is structured to address the following objectives (U.S. Department of Justice 2002, pp. 4)

1. Encourage greater coordination and cooperation among agencies and units of local government
2. Provide clearer objectives and priorities
3. Improve the analysis and understanding of crime and criminal justice problems
4. Solidify effective resource allocation
5. Develop quality criminal justice programs and personnel.
6. Improve the quality of justice

At the local justice system level, planning is designed to assist department heads and elected officials, such as county judge, county administrator, county commissioners, sheriff, district attorney and judiciary and corrections personnel. It is important at this level to provide an organizational climate that would be conducive to maintaining cooperation and coordination among *constitutionally separate* government agencies. At the community level, planning is structured by including organizations such as municipal law enforcement agencies, municipal court judges, bail bondsmen, defense lawyers, and certain community representatives. Additional planning and coordination at the system wide level is occasionally required in order to coordinate issues that arise with federal, regional, or state justice agencies.

The follow is an example of a criminal justice coordinating committee addressing jail overcrowding. A committee may be charged with the responsibility to review existing policies and programs that are directly or indirectly related to jail population, and/or develop new policies or programs; but with the requirement to utilize a collaborative system-wide effort with criminal justice agencies. The following is an overview of this strategy.

Jail Focus Group: The Jail Focus Group goal is to meet and address system wide issues related to jail population such as:

1. Expeditious processing of jail population
2. Pretrial release operations
3. Study jail population and capacity
4. Assess system issues associated with the arrest through filing of a court case
5. The development of criminal court case flow processes and docket management systems
6. The process associated with court-appointed lawyers and indigent defense process
7. The records management process related to the judgment, sentencing, and indictment process
8. State parole revocations

9. State prisoner transfer requirements
10. The continuous evaluation of existing programs that have a positive impact on jail population

Focus groups of this type may include representatives from area municipalities, county administration, county jail administrator, county attorney, judiciary, probation, county clerk's office parole division, and information technology.

Some states have fostered the formation of local Criminal Justice Coordinating Committees (CJCC) either through comprehensive criminal justice planning bodies or through community corrections legislation. The following jurisdictions, listed alphabetically by county name and population, identify their local criminal justice planning groups as criminal justice coordinating committees, councils or commissions (U.S. Department of Justice 1999):

1.   Hennepin County, Minnesota (1,116,200)
2.   Jefferson County, Colorado (527,056)
3.   Jefferson County, Kentucky (693,604)
4.   Los Angeles County, California (9,519,338)
5.   Lucas County, Ohio (455,054)
6.   Marion County, Oregon (284,834)
7.   Multnomah County, Oregon (660,486)
8.   Palm Beach County, Florida (1,131,184)
9.   San Mateo County, California (707,161)
10.   Sarasota County, Florida (325,957)

Oregon and Colorado are two states that have developed comprehensive CJCCs. These states built on the success of the community corrections acts that required states and local partnerships to improve local corrections operations. Maryland, Pennsylvania, and Virginia have statewide initiatives that promote collaboration across justice system components and focus on concerns and priorities at the community level (National Criminal Justice Association 1998). Similar programs are also found in the form of adjudication partnerships in Buffalo, New York; Los Angeles County; Cedar Rapids; Iowa, San Jose, California; Dakota County, Minnesota; and Corvallis, Oregon (U.S. Department of Justice 1999).

Sociology Reference:

Functionalist's Perspective: The concept of power is not a matter of social coercion and domination but instead flows from a social system's potential to *coordinate* human activity and resources in order to accomplish goals. For example, from this perspective the power of the State rests on a *consensus* of values and interests in the name of which the State acts towards the greater benefit of all.

Negotiated Order: The power structure in an organization is not a fixed feature of organizational life to which people conform in a predictable and mechanical way. Instead, it is a result of on ongoing process of negotiation, bargaining, and compromise out of which the actual distribution of power emerges, takes shape, and changes over time. Negotiated order theory provides a useful tool for *cooperative planning* among organizations, which may be the best approach for addressing shared problems. Organizations can negotiate the terms of their future interactions with one another, and in so doing mold their interorganizational (IO) fields. *The Journal of Applied Behavioral Science,* Vol. 27, No. 2, (1991): pp.163-180

Works Cited

National Criminal Justice Association 1998. Community-Based Planning: *Promoting a Neighborhood Response to Crime Policy and Practice*

U.S Department of Justice, National Institute of Corrections, *Guidelines for Developing a Criminal Justice Coordinating Committee* (January, 2002) **http://www.nicic.org/pubs/2002/017232.pdf** (accessed June 2, 2007)

U. S. Department of Justice, Office of Justice Programs, *Key Elements of Successful Adjudication Partnerships,* May 1999 (on-line serial), Bureau of Justice Assistance, NCJ 173949:1.

STEP 7

AN ANALYSIS MODEL THAT MEASURES THE PERFORMANCE OF THE CRIMINAL JUSTICE SYSTEM

As previously indicated, it is important for you to understand that *doing justice* implies at least four things: holding offenders fully accountable for their offenses, protecting offenders' constitutional and legal rights, treating like offenses alike, and taking into account relevant differences among offenders and offenses (U.S. Department of Justice 1993). The end result of "doing justice" is improved community safety, victim services, social justice, and a reduction in recidivism. Therefore, it is necessary to have an analysis model that measures the performance of the criminal justice system.

The effectiveness of sentences, programs, and community, using reduced recidivism as a measure of success, is at the heart of virtually every examination of recidivism because everyone wants to know what works. Researchers and policy analysts have struggled with this problem for decades, and it will not be solved in this discussion.

The public's desire to reduce the economic and social costs associated with crime and incarceration has resulted in an emphasis on recidivism as a measure of program effectiveness. While few would deny either the intrinsic value of education or the significance of other outcomes, correctional education's ability to keep individuals from re-entering the criminal justice system will ultimately win or lose supporters and funding.

Measuring recidivism requires considerable planning and commitment. A good recidivism study rules out the possibility that other factors (e.g., participant characteristics, participation in another program, post-release support activities) explain the observed outcomes. A good recidivism study includes some type of *comparison or control group* so that comparisons can be made between those who participate in correctional education and those who do not.

A review of the research on recidivism reveals a variety of different ways to define and measure this concept. Three different measurement dimensions that need to be considered are the precipitating event, the element of time, and the facility. The following information was obtained from an on-line serial entitled

Using Correctional Education Data: Issues and Strategies, January 1997.
http://www.ed.gov/offices/OVAE/AdultEd/OCE/IssuesStrategies/ch5.html

1. The precipitating event refers to the activity that ultimately determines whether or not a former inmate is considered a recidivist. Some research uses the *revocation of parole* as the precipitating event, other studies use *re-arrest,* and still others use reconviction. Some studies have also examined whether the seriousness of the crime for which the individual was *reconvicted* was greater or lesser than the previous conviction.

2. The second measurement dimension is the length of time between release from prison and the precipitating event. Obviously, the longer the period of time between the release and return dates, the greater the likelihood that former inmates will have recidivated. Some evaluations have used six months as an initial cutoff after release while others go indefinitely. Most evaluations limit the time period being examined; one to two years after release is a reasonable length of time to use.

3. The third measurement dimension that needs to be considered in measuring recidivism, if the precipitating event determining recidivism is violation of parole or reconviction, is the facility to which the individual returns. If programs are only interested in determining whether former inmates return to the facility from which they were released, data collection becomes relatively easy. This means that the program does not need to link their records to those of other prisons or systems within the state or elsewhere in the nation. This is problematic because limiting definitions of recidivism to a single facility can produce misleading results.

Three Dimensions of a Recidivism Measure

- Precipitation event
- Time- release and return
- Readmitting facility

A study released by the U.S. Department of Justice in June 2002, titled *Recidivism of Prisoners Released in 1994* can be used as an example for the development of standardized recidivism measures. It was found that nearly 300,000 prisoners released in 15 States in 1994, sixty-seven percent were rearrested within 3 years. This same study delineated that in 1983 releases estimated sixty-two percent. Released prisoners with the highest re-arrest rates were robbers (70.2 percent), burglars (74.0 percent), larcenists (74.6 percent), motor vehicle thieves (78.8 percent), those in prison for possessing or selling stolen property (77.4 percent), and those in prison for possessing, using, or selling illegal weapons (70.2 percent).

The study used four measures of recidivism: rearrest, reconviction, re-sentence to prison, and return to prison with or without a new sentence. Three of the recidivism measures, re-arrest, re-conviction, and re-sentence to prison are based exclusively on official criminal records kept in State and FBI criminal history repositories. One recidivism measure, return to prison with or without a new prison sentence, is formed from a combination of records from criminal history repositories plus prison records kept by State departments of corrections. The information below is an excerpt from the above study explaining the three levels of recidivism measures.

1. Re- Arrest: Within three years of their release in 1994, 61.7 percent of offenders sentenced for violence were arrested for a new offense. Arrest records provide an incomplete measure of actual criminal activity because people are sometimes arrested for crimes they did not commit. Research also indicates that offenders commit more crimes than their arrest records show. (Blumstein, 1986)

2. Re-Convicted: Within the first year of release, an estimated 21.5 percent of the 272,111 released offenders were reconvicted for a new felony or misdemeanor; within the first 2 years, a combined total of 36.4 percent were reconvicted; and within the first 3 years, a combined total of 46.9 percent were reconvicted. It is necessary to note that not all of the reconvicted prisoners were re-sentenced to another prison term for their new crime. Some were sentenced to confinement in a local jail. Some were sentenced to neither prison nor jail but to probation, which allowed them to remain free in their communities but under the supervision of a probation officer.

3. Returned to Prison: Within the first year of release, 10.4 percent of the 272,111 released prisoners were RETURNED back in prison as a result of a conviction and prison sentence for a new crime; within the first 2 years, 18.8 percent; and within the first 3 years, 25.4 percent.

Sociology Reference:

Measurement: Measurement is a key process in sociological research through which we observe the world and record the results for interpretation and analysis. In order to do this, we need a set of procedures that specifies exactly how to observe.

Experiment: An experiment is a scientific research method used to establish cause-and-effect relationships between variables. In its simplest form, the experiment compares two groups of observations under two conditions that are identical in every respect but one. The experimental group is exposed to a condition believed to have some kind of causal effect. The control group is not exposed to that condition.

Variable: A variable is any measurable characteristic that differs from one observation to another. When explaining the causal relationship between variables, the variable to be explained is called dependent, while the variable believed to produce an effect is called independent.

Reliability: Reliability is the degree to which a measurement instrument gives the *same results each time* it is used, assuming that the underlying think being measured does not change.

Validity: Validity is the degree to which a measurement instrument such as a *survey question* measures what we in fact think it measures.

Works Cited

Blumstein A., et. al. 1986. Criminal Careers and "Career Criminals," vol. 1, pp.55.Washington, DC: National Academy Press.

Using Correctional Education Data: Issues and Strategies, January 1997, [On-Line   Serial] **http://www.ed.gov/offices/OVAE/AdultEd/OCE/IssuesStrategies/ch5.html**

U.S. Department of Justice, Bureau of Justice Statistics, *Performance Measures for the Criminal Justice System* October 1993, (NCJ-143505)

U.S. Department of Justice, Bureau of Justice Statistics, *Recidivism of Prisoners Released in 1994,* June 2002 [On-line serial] NCJ 193427, pp. 1-16.

STEP 8

MONITOR THE ORGANIZATIONAL ENVIRONMENT

Presuming that you are a student of criminal justice, it is equally important to become familiar with the language of sociology. The language of sociology is what sociologists use to study social life. It is this language that takes us beyond merely seeing what is all around us, to noticing, to paying attention in ways that enable us to understand social life in a more systematic way (Johnson 2000). The criminal justice system's organizational environment is social life and can be described as any external phenomenon, event, group, or individual that is composed of cultural, ecological, economic, political, legal, technological, and demographic forces (Kolfas et al. 1990). Kolfas affirmed that as environmental conditions change, demands for service, legal resources positions on policy and programs of both public and private organizations may change (pp.19). Kolfas further explained that these new demands, constraints, and pressures *may alter the mission* or policy of the organization (pp.19). For example, increasing the number of arrests as a result of an increase in crime and public pressure will impact the criminal justice system. The populations of *jails will increase* [1] and court dockets and caseloads of prosecuting attorneys will expand (pp. 29). There are many variables that impact jail and prison populations and most correctional agencies are without an internal jail population projection process. It is important that a long-term research and planning model is developed that addresses all variables that may impact jail population and is considered apolitical and empirically based (Appendix B). Additional variables that impact the organization are through direct pressures from constituents and clients and indirectly through governmental action (pp.25). The government's response to political conditions can be passed on to the organization and other agencies within the system. Governments can be influenced to change budgets, and mandates, and alter the composition of top administrative personnel. These situations normally result after elections or legislation is written that changes the purpose or power base of a bureaucracy (pp. 25).

Changes in organizational environments have led to a variety of justice models being used over the years. Cole (1998) identifies seven justice models used from the 1600s through the 1990's: the Colonial, Penitentiary, Reformatory, Progressive, Medical, Community, and Crime Control models (pp.456). For example, as the political climate changed in the 1970's and 1980's, a renewed emphasis on the crime control model of corrections developed. The crime control model [2] emphasizes efficiency and the capacity to catch, try, convict, and punish a high proportion of offenders; it also stresses speed and finality over the possibility that innocent people might be adversely impacted. (Cole et al.1998 pp. 9). All of these factors have led to disproportionate *increases in jail population.*

The crime control model focuses on counting activities such as response time, arrests, convictions and the numbers of those receiving correctional services yet it fails to effectively address "results," such as reductions in crime, recidivism, and jail populations as a component of the total system outcomes. The development of a more coordinated, apolitical and non-competing justice model is the key that will let it protect itself from the forces of the organizational environment. These are not "simple solutions," but challenging goals as we move away from a preoccupation with the one-dimensional approach to criminal justice, which has led to unprecedented levels of recidivism and jail populations.

Sociology Reference:

Environment: In general, an environment is any set of things, forces, or conditions in relation to which something exists or takes place. A social environment includes both material culture (such as buildings and computers) and the abstract cultural and structural characteristics of social systems that constrain and shape the terms on which social life is lived.

Social Evolution: Social evolution may be considered a process through which societies develop in predictable ways that generally reflect progress toward higher or more nearly perfect forms of social life. Social evolution may also consist of unilinear change that follows a prescribed path, for example, simpler to more complex forms of social organization.

Works Cited

Cole, G. F. and C.E. Smith 1998 *The American System of Criminal Justice,* 8, 22-40, 143-257, 456.

Hahn, P.H. 1998 *Emerging Trends in Criminal Justice,* pp.10-11, pp. 158-160, 162, 166., Thousand Oaks, California, Sage Publications

Johnson, Allan G., 2000 *The Blackwell Dictionary of Sociology* 2nd edition, Malden, Massachusetts, Blackwell Publishers Inc.

Kolfas, J.S. S. Stojkovic and D. Kalinich 1990, Defining the environment of the criminal justice system. *Criminal Justice Organizations Administration and Management,* pp. 18-30. Belmont, CA: Wadsworth

NOTES

1.   A *jail population projection model* includes many variables associated with the organizational environment and is considered an effective barometer of social conditions, therefore it is suggested that you to develop a multi-dimensional evaluation model that that not only addresses jail population but the entire organizational environment. This approach may provide you with additional information about the community that may have been missed otherwise such as income and poverty rates, educational levels of citizens, available housing, employment rates, and other factors that may lead to social disadvantage and crime (Appendix B). And since criminal justice organizations as well as their employees are impacted by changes in the organizational environment, there is also a need for an *organization survey* to monitor each department within the criminal justice system, in order to evaluate organizational change. Step 11 addresses this survey.

2.   Herbert Packer (1968) in his article titled *The Limits of the Criminal Sanction* "Two Models of the Criminal Process" (pp. 149-173) explains that the crime control model competes with the due process model, a model that encourages the adversarial process, the rights of defendants, and formal decision-making processes. He emphasizes that no one official agency functions according to one mode or the other and elements of both models are found throughout the system. However, as indicated above, the crime control model has been identified as the predominant model, resulting in a philosophy that encourages police and prosecutors to decide early on whether the defendant is innocent or guilty. This may result in more procedural errors.

STEP 9

A PLANNING PROCESS AT THE GOVERNMENT AND COMMUNITY LEVEL

It is important for you to have a planning process established at the government and community level, structured to improve the effective administration of justice. Planning can be defined as a decision-making process that involves politics and an effort to accomplish goals by increasing awareness and understanding of the decision making process (Dahl 1959, pp.340-350). The politics of planning is the total behavior of the political order within which planning takes place. For example, to understand politics of fiscal planning in the United States, one needs to understand the political processes of the United States. Therefore, planning is regarded as a rational social action and as a *social process* for reaching a rational decision (Dahl 1959). Therefore, it can be inferred by this premise that to understand the politics of state criminal justice planning, one needs to understand the *politics* of planning at the state, county and local levels in order to facilitate an effective decision-making process.

Local and state criminal justice systems are constantly under pressure to plan more efficiently and effectively without diminishing the quality of their services (U.S. Department of Justice 1999). Problems associated with backlogged dockets, crowded jails, and *recidivism* are becoming commonplace. Collaborative efforts are becoming more important for mounting an efficient and effective response to these problems (U.S. Department of Justice 1999 pp.1). The creation of a cooperative planning partnership with independent agencies, although an arduous task for many jurisdictions; has emerged as one of the solutions to improve communication among these agencies in order to deal with such complex issues (U.S. Department of Justice 1999).

The following characteristics are considered important ingredients for the development of successful collective planning and decision making partnerships that are deemed *consensus* builders (U.S. Department of Justice 1999):

1. Leadership: Key individuals in the organization must provide *leadership* to give direction. Leaders from one or more key agencies must step forward to assemble a team of leaders and managers that are concerned about issues facing their jurisdiction.

2. Research and Evaluation: This group of individuals (i.e., steering committee) must use research information on the *best practices* to guide program development as well as the use of objective data to evaluate its programs.

3. Broad Support: Partnerships of this type must seek *community* support. These partnerships must provide information about the focus of their group and improve the communication process by seeking community input on identifying and addressing problems.

In criminal justice organizations, justice leaders have been successful in bringing together key players to tackle difficult problems (U.S. Department of Justice 1999, pp. 2). Adjudication partnerships have been organized that include representatives from primary players in the adjudication process: the prosecution, the defense, and the court. The participation of other criminal justice agencies such as law enforcement and corrections are also included (U.S. Department of Justice 1999 pp. 2). Through a national mail survey, 103 well-established and successful partnerships of this type were identified (U.S. Department of Justice 1999 pp.4-8). These programs were found in Buffalo, New York; Los Angeles County; Cedar Rapids, Iowa; Dakota County, Minnesota; Rochester, New York; San Jose, California; and Corvallis, Oregon. Oregon, Nebraska, and Washington State have the best examples of City-County and State committees. These coalitions are examples of criminal justice planning groups that have been deemed successful for many years. It was also found that *community* can be a significant influence in shaping criminal justice policy and that new planning strategies should be developed that include collaborative efforts on behalf of the community and justice agencies (U.S. Department of Justice BJA 1997).

For many years, the community as an environmental force has failed to be an influence on the criminal justice system (U.S. Department of Justice BJA, 1997 pp.1). The police, prosecution, courts, and corrections systems have become increasingly modernized in recent years, but they often fail to meet the needs of the justice system's primary consumers: the communities that experience crime problems on a daily basis (e.g., U.S. Department of Justice 1997 BJA pp.1) This problem was first addressed by the advocates of community-based policing. They argued that police officers could address crime problems more effectively if they established closer relationships with the community. As a result of these efforts, community-based policing became a reality and these community-based planning concepts of "community justice" have spread to other branches of the justice system, including courts, probation departments, prosecutors, and corrections offices (U.S. Department of Justice BJA,1997 pp.1) The literature suggests that as local concerns grow about the offender's eventual return to the community and recidivism, the community and community justice planning groups are beginning to have a greater influence in shaping criminal justice policy.

Many local governments are finding that comprehensive system-wide planning (interagency and cross-jurisdictional) through the use of criminal justice coordinating committees helps to streamline the local system of justice, improve communication, eliminate duplication, fills service gaps, and generally improves the quality of services while controlling costs. These efforts will require coordination of city, county, regional, state, federal, and private justice agency activities (U.S. Department of Justice 2002, pp. 9-10). (Refer to the following Web pages for additional information on criminal justice coordinating committees: **http://www.nicic.org/pubs/2002/017232.pdf http://www.ncjrs.gov/pdffiles/173391.pdf http://nicic.org/Library/020972.**

In order to effectively achieve these aforementioned planning goals, it is necessary to establish a governance structure that includes collaboration between the community and representatives from each component of the criminal justice system: law enforcement, prosecution, courts and corrections. This governance structure or charter supports the criminal justice coordinating committee by providing the direction and commitment necessary to develop a criminal justice plan and address the criminal justice system's goals and objectives. The charter also serves as the governing instrument for the project. It defines the scope of the project, the management structure, and the roles and responsibilities of its membership. Project groups and teams operate in many different ways depending on project objectives, technical needs, and resource requirements and availability. The project charter establishes the manner in which these groups and teams are structured by defining the functions, expectations, and accountability of members of the team. These guidelines minimize the risk that the project will be derailed as the result of error, misunderstanding, or miscommunication. A charter includes the following components:

1. Vision, Mission, and Principles
2. Background
3. Project Definition
4. Project Description
5. Project Outcomes and Objectives
6. Project Deliverables
7. Scope
8. Project Constraints and Assumptions
9. Project Approach
10. Research Design
11. Service Delivery Design
12. Activity Timeline
13. Project Participants
14. Issues and Risks
15. Project Management

Refer to this Web page for an example of a project charter:
http://www.vita.virginia.gov/projects/cpm/templates/project-charter-template-1.3.doc

Sociology Reference:

Social Contract: A social contract is an idea that has been used as a metaphor to describe the sharing of authority within a collaborative relationship between *citizens and the state* primarily for community safety and self protection.

Works Cited

Dahl, R.A. 1959 The Politics of Planning, *International Social Science Journal*, 24:340-350

U. S. Department of Justice, Office of Justice Programs, [On-Line Serial] May 1999 *Key Elements of Successful Adjudication Partnerships,* Bureau of Justice Assistance NCJ 173949, pp. 1-11.

U. S. Department of Justice, Bureau of Justice Assistance, November 1997 [On-Line serial], *Responding to the Community: Principles for Planning Creating a Community Court,* Bureau of Justice Assistance, NCJ 166821, pp.1.

U.S. Department of Justice, January 2002, *Guidelines for Developing a Criminal Justice Coordinating Committee.*

STEP 10

CRIMINAL JUSTICE ADMINISTRATORS SHOULD UNDERSTAND THE CAUSES OF CRIME

A comprehensive understanding of the causes of anti-social behavior will assist you in future decision-making roles in order to effectively lead and manage an organization. Using assigned criminological theories, discussions address the development of antisocial behavior from birth to adulthood and the continuity that exists between juvenile and adult crime.

If your intentions are to begin a career in criminal justice or planning, it is necessary to understand the underlying causes of crime. Many programs exist today that offer rehabilitative and reintegration value if the *criminogenesis* process is identified. It is important to have a general understanding of criminological theory, social justice issues and the risk factor approaches to identifying antisocial behavior. The information below is a general overview of various criminological theories taken from text books titled *Theoretical Criminology 4th Edition,* 1998, New York, Oxford University Press, by Vold, Bernard and Snipes and *Social Deviance, 1994,* Nedham Heights, MA, Allyn and Bacon, by Ward, Carter and Perrin.

Criminological Theory [1]

Classical Criminology: Crime is seen as a product of the free choice of the individual, who assesses the potential benefits of committing the crime against its potential costs.

Positivist Criminology: Behavior is determined by factors beyond the individual's control. Humans are not self-determined agents free to do as they wish and as their intelligence directs.

Psychoanalytic Explanations: Freud himself did not discuss criminal behavior to any great extent. He did, however, suggest that at least some individuals performed criminal acts because they possessed an overdeveloped superego (primarily an unconscious reservoir of social experience), which led to constant feelings of guilt and anxiety. There is a constant desire for punishment to remove guilt feelings and restore a proper balance of good against evil.

Crime and Economic Conditions: Both poverty and inequality are clearly associated with crime, especially violent crime, but whether they cause crime is another matter. At present a stronger case can be made that the level of general economic inequality in a society (i.e., the gap between its wealthiest and its poorest citizens) has a causal impact on the level of violent crime in that society.

Labeling Theories: The process by which audience reactions, in the form of sanctions and stigmatizing labels, serve to increase the behaviors complained of. Therefore, there is a link between societal reactions and criminal careers.

Critical Criminology: Karl Marx believed that it is essential to human nature that people be productive in life and in work. But in industrialized capitalist societies there are large numbers of unemployed and underemployed people. Because these people are unproductive, they become demoralized and are subject to all forms of crime and vice.

Spiritual Explanations: Spiritual explanations of crime are part of a general view of life in which many events are believed to result from the influence of otherworldly powers. For example, some religious individual and groups still attribute crime to the influence of the devil. Charles Colson, who was special counsel to President Richard M. Nixon and who served seven months in prison for his part in the Watergate affair, attributes crime to sinful human nature. He argues that religious conversion is the only "cure" for crime and spends much of his time bringing that Christian message to prisoners.

Human Ecological Theory: There is developing literature that provides explicitly evolutionary and ecological discussions of crime, found in the writings of Cohen, Machalek, Vila, Ekblom, ElHs, Walsh, and others. These make explicit links between human nature, ecology, and crime, combining both deeper ecological analyses and what often is referred to as either evolutionary psychology or, in anthropology, cultural evolution. For example, Cohen and Machalek (1988) introduced a theory of expropriative behavior (theft) based on principles from evolution and ecology. Their contributions include the insight that using the behavioral strategy as the unit of analysis may help us understand the normality of crime as originally observed by Durkheim. Cohen and Machalek cast humans as behavioral strategists, comparing them to bees, eagles, and other species and distinguishing them as more intelligent, more prone to use cultural transmission of behavior, and keener at recognizing opportunities to devise new strategies than other types of organisms. They point out that the usefulness of any particular behavioral strategy for acquiring desired resources depends on the *frequency* with which that strategy is being used in the population as a whole. They also suggest that "resource holding asymmetries" (differences between individuals in attributes or resources that enable them to acquire and retain resources) can help explain why some individuals are more likely to use expropriation as a strategy for obtaining resources. In essence, they predict that highly disadvantaged individuals will tend to use expropriation to make the best of a bad situation while highly advantaged individuals might be tempted to use expropriation to take advantage of a good situation.

Social Justice Issues and Crime

Allan Johnson refers to justice as a concept of fairness and to the process of people getting what they deserve (Johnson 2005 pp.164). In a legal sense, for example, justice consists of treating everyone according to law, of guaranteeing civil rights, and following prescribed procedure in a consistent and evenhanded way. Distributive justice or social justice, however, involves less precise notions of what is fair, especially in the distribution of resources and rewards such as wealth. Is a just society, for example, one that guarantees equality of opportunity or equality of outcomes (pp. 164)?

Jeffrey Reiman argues that the criminal justice systems is not structured to reduce crime or achieve justice but to project to the American people a visible image of the threat of crime. (Reiman, 1996 pp.1) Reiman suggests that this is done by maintaining a sizable population of criminals while at the same time failing to reduce crime. Barry Glassner (1999) suggests that the threat of crime is found in what he has identified as the "culture of fear." Glassner explains that the price tag for *panic* about crime has grown so monumental that even law and order advocates find it difficult to defend. The criminal justice system costs Americans approximately $100 billion a year, most of which is allocated to po-lice and prisons, yet increases in the number of police officers and prison cells do not correlate consistently with a reduction in serious crime. Therefore, while fortunes are being allocated to protect our children from dangers that few ever encounter, approximately 11 million children lack health insurance, 12 million are living in poverty, and the rates of illiteracy are increasing (pp. xcii).

Extreme inequality is also associated with political instability and adverse outcomes for society as a whole. *Poverty* for example correlates strongly with child abuse, crime and drug abuse. [2] The larger the gap between the rich and the poor in a society, the higher its overall death rates from heart disease, cancer, murder.(p.xviii). Jeffrey Reiman suggests that we need to move to towards a system of criminal *justice* versus *criminal* justice. He urges policies that:

1. End crime-producing poverty
2. Create a correctional system that promotes human dignity
3. Make police, prosecution, courts and corrections more just
4. Establish economic and social justice
5. Criminalize the dangerous actions of the affluent and white-collar offenders

To complement Reiman's position, President Lyndon B. Johnson's Great Society agenda of 1963 addressed social justice by suggesting that "warring on poverty, inadequate housing, and unemployment is warring on crime"; "a civil rights law is a law against crime; and that money for schools is money against crime" (Kearns 1976).

The following information is a synopsis of social issues, such as those conditions that relate to economic status and that may lead to various levels of anti-social behavior, as well as strategies for action. This information was derived from the textbook entitled *Understanding Social Problems* Mooney, Linda A., David Knox, and Caroline Schacht, Chapters 7-10, p. 202-292.

Poverty and Economic Opportunity

• Where jobs are scarce residents may rely on illegitimate sources of income, i.e., the disappearance of work/jobs creates family dissolution, welfare, social disorganization, and crime.

• Culture of poverty/underclass: Gratification in the present and not the future because there is not a future. Lack of participation in society's major institutions. Feelings of powerless, inferiority, and personal unworthiness result in early sexual activity, joblessness, reliance on public assistance, illegitimate income-producing activities, and substance abuse.

• Approximately 32 million Americans live in poverty (approximately 12 percent)

• Discrimination in education, employment, income, housing, and politics against ethic minorities. For example, disparities in school funding, distortion of history in textbooks, median household income, promotions, job offers, and salaries. All are evidence of institutionalized discrimination.

• Institutional discrimination or social oppression: When its enforcement is so embedded in the everyday workings of social life, it is not easily identified as social oppression and does not require conscious prejudice or overt acts of discrimination .

• Employment discrimination and wealth. Whites that received an advanced level degree, bachelor degree, high school diploma, or no degree received higher annual salaries when compared to blacks and Hispanics. Hispanics received a higher annual salary than blacks with advanced degrees.

- Housing segregation and discrimination

- Political discrimination (i.e., voting irregularities in 2000 election)

- Racial and ethnic harassment in the workplace (hostile environment)

- Hate crimes

Strategies for Action

- Increase minority representation and participation in government, which will minimize distrust in government by the same (participation is increasing in the United States.);
- Maintain affirmative action programs, which is not restricted to minorities; it addresses Vietnam veterans, people with disabilities, and white woman.
- *Multicultural education* in schools and communities; diversity training.
- Reduce or eliminate disparities in school funding; in recent years more that two dozen states had to address disparities in school funding primarily those schools in poor districts and those serving minority students.
- Religious movement in the advancement of engaging with those of different races and ethnic groups for the purposes of advancing reconciliation.
- Social change will come from grassroots community and religious activists, striving to change the nature of society one community and one soul at a time.
- Alterations in the structure of society that increase "fairness" and opportunities for minorities in education, employment and income, and political participation are critical.
- Current policy-makers that are concerned must act to address these inequities and create opportunities
- Address these issues objectively, and omit indicating bigotry and individual prejudice and address class, gender and fundamental fairness.

Epidemiological Approach

If a disease was an issue and seriously threatened our lives and well being, we would do our best to eradicate this illness, rather than preparing secure facilities in which to quarantine those who have been affected. The National Center for Disease Control in Atlanta has consistently called for the use of an epidemiological/risk factor model to address the serious problems of juvenile violence in our society (Friday 1994) Hahn explains (1998) that the epidemiological model constitutes a more proactive approach to crime control because it includes:

1.   Identification of the problem - developing health surveillance systems that will allow us to measure, document and monitor the problem over time.

2.   Identification of the cause - Identifying the causes, or *risk factors*, so that we can design and implement preventative techniques.

3.   Development of testing of interventions that are based on information learned in the earlier stages. In other words, a controlled process of evaluation research that will show us what kinds of interventions will work and in what settings.

4.   Implementation of interventions and measurement of prevention effectiveness, applying field tested interventions, including education interventions. These may include public awareness campaigns offered in a real-world setting, with the opportunity to evaluate how they work, thus assuring their costs, consequences, and benefits.

The epidemiological model suggests that crime is not one-dimensional and requires a multidisciplinary approach if it is to be dealt with effectively. This, in turn, requires a more multidisciplinary and integrated crime control model. For example, the chain of *criminogenic issues begins in infancy* or even before birth, with poor medical care of the mother, and infant. It proceeds through the preschool years and into adulthood.

The Search Institute, is an independent nonprofit organization whose mission is to bring together community, state, and national leaders to address positive human development (**http://www.search-institute.org/assets/**). It lists 40 Developmental Assets that are concrete, common sense, positive experiences and qualities essential to raising successful young people. These assets have the power during critical adolescent years to influence choices young people make and help them become caring, responsible adults. The average young person the Search Institute surveyed experiences 18 of these assets. Overall, 62 percent of young people surveyed experience fewer than 20 of the assets. In short, most young people in the United States do not have in their lives many of the basic building blocks of healthy development. When they have more assets, young people are more likely to engage in positive behaviors. [2]

The National Center for Disease Control in Atlanta calls for the use of an epidemiological model to address the serious problems of juvenile violence in our society. This model constitutes a proactive approach to crime control. It establishes continuity between juvenile and adult violence. Violent behavior that begins before the eighteenth birthday normally continues throughout a lifetime (Hamparian, et al 1985). A study by Chaiken and Chaiken (1982, pp.15-17) revealed that most violent adults have tended to have:

1. Committed violent crimes before age 16

2. Committed violent crimes frequently as juveniles

3. Used drugs frequently as juveniles

4. Been convicted of a crime before age 16

5. Had multiple commitments to juvenile institutions

Although not all children who grow up in violent homes become violent, the position that violence results in more violence is valid, especially when it is experienced in childhood. Abuse in childhood encourages the victims to use aggression as a means to solving problems and normally prevents the individual from feeling empathy for others. Straus, Gelles, and Steinmetz (1980) found that over 20 percent of adults who had been *abused* as children later abused their own children (pp. 107-108). In another study (Widom 1989a), carefully controlled for age, sex and race, found that persons who had been *abused or neglected* as children had significantly greater likelihood of arrest for a violent offense than did persons in a control group (15 percent vs. 7.9 percent). Although not extensive, this step has identified and explained the underlying causes of antisocial behavior that can lead to a dysfunctional life and possibly crime.

Another approach to addressing the aforementioned issues is the use of a locally based social factor analysis. For example, Willoughby City, Australia uses a census-based system entitled *The Index of Relative Socio-Economic Disadvantage.* This system has been constructed using recent census data that identifies relatively disadvantaged areas within the community (e.g., areas with many low income earners) and assigns low to high index values. This index is derived from social attributes such as low income, low educational attainment, high unemployment, jobs in relatively unskilled occupations and variables that reflect disadvantage rather than measure specific aspects of disadvantage (e.g., Indigent and Separated/Divorced). Additional information on this system can be found at:
http://www.id.com.au/willoughby/commprofile/default.asp?id=234&pg=240

The City of Dallas, Texas, through the J. McDonald Williams Institute Foundation for Community Empowerment, developed a similar strategy entitled the Wholeness Index. Wholeness means that each person in a city enjoys an equally productive and satisfying life, regardless of where in the city he or she lives. In a whole city, residents of every part of town have an equal opportunity to achieve financial success, are equally self-sufficient, and are equally active in political and civic life. Disparity is the opposite of wholeness. The greater the disparities from one part of town to the other (in practice, often meaning from the richest to the poorest neighborhoods), the less whole the city is. The Williams Institute and the Foundation for Community Empowerment believes that wholeness is the fundamental measure of a city's (or a nation's) success; wholeness is a moral and political imperative, but data strongly suggests that it is also an economic imperative. That is, cities and regions with *less disparity* enjoy better overall economic growth and *spend less on prisons (i.e., crime)*, emergency medical care, and other band-aids for disparity than those that are less whole. The following categories are evaluated by the Wholeness Institute.

1. Index Crime Rate
2. Wealth
3. School Holding Power
4. Life Span
5. Voter Turnout
6. Families Not In Poverty
7. Owner Occupancy
8. Access to Retail
9. Graduation Rate
10. Fit Housing
11. SAT Scores
12. Middle-Class Housing

Additional information on this strategy can be found at: **http://www.thewilliamsinstitute.org/**

Sociological References:

Epidemiology: When epidemiology is combined with a sociological perspective, it raises questions about the connection between the life of human beings as biological organisms and cultural and structural characteristics of social systems. For example: The fact that cigarette smoking is more prevalent among lower and working classes suggests the relationship between social class and the distribution of life-enhancing and/or self-destructive behaviors.

Socialization: A process through which people come to identify with a social system and its values and norms, and thereby acquire a stake in maintaining these as well as their sense of belonging to the system. There is a fundamental belief that if social systems and norms are legitimate they are binding on its participants. (i.e., supportive or non-supportive communities).

Labeling Theory: Efforts at social control can backfire to produce more rather than less deviance. If people who steal, for example, are *labeled* thieves, imprisoned in the company of others who have stolen, shunned upon their release, and denied opportunities to work because they are not trusted, they likely will find themselves in a position in which further stealing is a practical necessity that fits the generally accepted view of who they are.

Social Darwinism: Regarding social inequality, social Darwinism attributed the gap between the wealth and poor primarily to the greater "fitness" of the wealthy survive and thrive. Society is ruled by competition and the principle of "survival of fittest," a phrase coined by Herbert Spencer.

Stratification and Inequality: Stratification is the social process through which rewards and resources such as wealth, power, and prestige are distributed systematically and unequally within our social systems.

Social Oppression: Social oppression is a concept that describes a relationship of dominance and subordination between categories of people in which one benefits from the systemic abuse, exploitation, and injustice directed toward the other. The relationship between whites and blacks in the United States and South Africa and between social classes in many industrial societies, between men and women in most societies, all have elements of social oppression in that the organization of social life enables those who dominate to oppress others.

Poverty: In general, poverty is a condition in which people lack what they need to live; but the "need to live" is a matter of definition. Absolute poverty is what people need to survive. Relative poverty is how much people have relative to other people in their society and culture (e.g., in parts of the world indoor plumbing is regarded and as a sign of affluence; but in industrial societies it is taken for granted). However, most theories of poverty focus on the characteristics of the poor, rather that the relationship between poverty and the great accumulations of wealth found in most capitalist societies.

Social Justice: A concept that involves less precise notions of what is fair, especially in the distribution of resources and rewards such as wealth. Is a just society one that guarantees equality of opportunity or equality of outcomes?

Notes

1. This list of various criminological theories is taken from texts: *Theoretical Criminology* by Vold, Bernard and Snipes and *Social Deviance* by Ward, Carter and Perrin.

2. Poverty, for example, correlates strongly with child abuse, crime and drug abuse. Also, the larger the gap between the rich and the poor in a society, the

higher its overall death rates from heart disease, cancer, and murder. Barry Glassner (1999) *The Culture of Fear*, Basic Books, p. xvii-xix.

3. It should be noted that because socially strained communities contribute to higher levels of crime, this index can also be used for identifying suitable environments and/or living conditions for the ex-offender population in order to minimize recidivism rates.

Works Cited

Chaiken, J.M., and M.R. Chaiken 1982. *Varieties of criminal behavior*, Santa Monica, CA: Rand Corporation pp.15-17

Cohen, L. E. and R. Machalek. 1988. "A general theory of expropriative crime" *American Journal of Sociology* 94:465-501

Friday J.C. 1994. "Violence Prevention From A Public Health Perspective: The U.S. Experience." *Miami Medicine*, January Issue: 64:15

Glassner, Barry. 1999. *The Culture of Fear*, pp. xvii xix. New York, NY Basic Books.

Hahn, P.H. 1998. *Emerging Trends in Criminal Justice*, 32, 34 39. Thousand Oaks, California, Sage Publications

Hamperian, D.M., J.M. Davis, J.M. Jacobson, and R.E. McGraw (1985) *The Young Criminal Years of the Violent Few.* Washington, DC: National Institute for Juvenile Justice and Delinquency Prevention.

Johnson, Allan G., 2005 *The Blackwell Dictionary of Sociology* 2nd edition, Inc. Malden, Massachusetts, Blackwell Publishers Inc.

Kearns, Doris. 1976 *Lyndon Johnson and the American Dream, pp. 216* New York: Harper & Row.

Mooney, Linda A. David Cox, and Caroline Schacht *Understanding Social Problems*, Chapters 7-10, pp. 202-292.

Reiman, J. 1996.....*And the Poor Get Prison: Economic Bias in American Criminal Justice System,* Needham Heights, MA: Allyn and Bacon.

Savage, Joanne and Bryan Vila. 2003, "Human Ecology, Crime, and Crime Control: Linking Individual Behavior and Aggregate Crime", *Social Biology,*

Spring Issue.

Straus, M.A., R.J. Gelles and S. K. Steinmetz 1980 Behind Closed Doors: *Violence in the American Family,* Garden City, New York: Doubleday.

Widom, Cathy S. 1989a "The cycle of violence", *Science,* 244, 160-166

STEPS 11&12

EVALUATE ORGANIZATIONAL NEEDS AND MOTIVATIONS WITHIN THE CONTEXT OF THE ORGANIZATIONAL MISSION

The need to view the criminal justice system as one systemic organizational unit is addressed again, as well as the need for you to evaluate the organization and the motivational strategies needed for organizational growth. It is emphasized that justice administrators must utilize fundamental management practices that will assist in meeting the overall goals of the criminal justice system. The argument is whether justice administrators are prepared to manage their organizations and motivate their employees to meet these goals by utilizing evaluative research in order to more effectively predict which needs and motivations seem to be more important than others.

If you are interested in improving or maintaining the health of an organization or have belonged to an ailing organization, you have felt the frustration associated with this condition. However, many of us are not trained in diagnosing the problem. To properly diagnose what is happening in an organization, you should consider applying the medical model as a strategy. The doctor evaluates the patient's symptoms, conducts an examination, and recommends a prescription for the ailing individual. Diagnosing problems within organizations is the same. The first step is to recognize that a problem exists. Doctors call them symptoms; Organizations call them problems. These problems may be associated with productivity, morale, communication, or other group-related problems.

If you have similar issues in your organization, they may be serious enough to invest time and resources; therefore, it is time to decide what actions and resources are needed to assess and diagnose the problem. People as patients and organizations as clients often self-diagnose. People consider simplistic remedies; organizations may send a few people to a seminar and put on some training programs once they return. This works only if you want symptomatic relief. Unfortunately, the underlying causes haven't been evaluated and changed, so the problem won't go away.

Certainly, the organizational changes needed must be addressed by the employees and their management; in other words, the patient has to take his medicine. However, resources may be needed outside the organization to objectively assess the problems and provide guidance on treatment options. Whoever this outside resource is, s/he should be politically neutral, knowledgeable in organizational assessment, and able to give guidance on the many treatment options. This person should speak frankly and communicate the problems that your employees feel but are hesitant to say.

If you have an ailing organization, it implies that organizational systems are a primary cause of the symptoms. Organizational systems such as the organizational structure, compensation, management style, employee performance, communication patterns, as well as organizational mission, vision, and goals are *major* and often overlooked causes of organizational ill health.

If you are attempting to modify or completely change the mission of the criminal justice organization, it is important to view the criminal justice system as a single organization. For example, if you choose community *justice* as the new mission each organizational sub-unit (i.e., police, prosecution, courts and corrections) is a vehicle that you may use in order to achieve this goal. Therefore, in order to meet this new mission, it is suggested to link it to each component of the criminal justice system. In turn, each criminal justice department must coordinate the development of individual mission statements for their departments and correlate their performance goals and objectives accordingly. Therefore, there are two important questions for the criminal justice administrator to answer before attempting this task: Am I currently addressing organizational needs; and, do I as an administrator, adequately have a managerial strategy in place to process these needs? While most administrators are usually aware of individual differences that are present in the workforce, better administrators make an effort to evaluate and predict which needs and motivations seem to be more important than others.

By effectively revealing the perceptions of both the manager and the employee, organizations can address their mission more effectively, and significantly increase their communication process and efficacy. This is primarily because administrators in accord with worker needs become more effective at managing their employees and in turn, employee performance improves. Therefore, it is important to *assess* the organization on a regular basis. An effective tool to use to address these issues is an employee perception survey. Typically, a survey reveals information that may not be readily apparent. For example, the kinds of things that workers indicate they want most from their jobs are not the same things that their manager often perceives as important. Many managers do not fully understand that what people want from their job actually changes across their time as an employee of a particular organization. Therefore, the purpose of the evaluation is to assess the needs and perceptions of employees and managers in order to better understand these needs and perceptions[1] within the context of the *organizational mission.* This knowledge allows managers to make educated decisions and adjustments regarding changes in the organizational environment, performance, workloads, job descriptions and expectations, etc. The point is that once the managers are in tune with the organizational environment they will have the knowledge to effectively create and manage their organizations. This enlightened workplace will motivate and satisfy all of its members, at all need levels.

For example, in an article addressing organizational change, which appeared in the *Fort Worth Star Telegram* on April 1, 2007, Dallas County District Attorney Craig Watkins stated that he is changing the mission of the District Attorney's Office. As he explained, the Dallas County District Attorney's Office will focus more on *justice than convictions*. Watkins articulated a vision that calls for strong punishment for hardened criminals but includes room for diversion programs, intervention, and a community court system. In order to achieve this new mission Watkins is changing the organizational hierarchy. In a single day, Watkins requested the resignations of eight of the highest ranking members of the department. Although these actions may be considered necessary, they may also impact employee/employer perceptions and if not addressed properly could impede the organizational mission. There are 284 members of the Dallas County District Attorney's Office. After changes of this magnitude occur, it is important to evaluate the employees' perceptions of this transformation, in order to ensure all that it remains within the context of the organizational mission.

Although there are many management strategies that suggest improvements in organizational effectiveness, I suggest that you conduct *organizational assessments* on a regular basis that incorporates three dominant organizational theories used by leading managers throughout the country: 1) Maslow's Hierarchy of Needs theory; 2) Herzberg's Motivation Hygiene theory; and 3) Lindahl's theory on "What Workers Want From Their Jobs". In short, Maslow proposes that levels of human needs must be addressed in a specific order before a person feels satisfied, while Herzberg suggests that motivational factors within the job itself satisfy the employee more than environmental and/or maintenance factors surrounding the job. Lindhal further specifies these ideas by suggesting that managerial perceptions are typically different from those of the employees. The survey instrument utilized in this evaluation process uses these three organizational theories by including questions that quickly and effectively evaluate human needs and motives, employee goals and incentives, and individual differences. This survey creates an empirical measurement that can serve as the basis for current and future policy decisions.

This assessment process allows you to better understand how employees and managers view their jobs and the value of their work. It can be used as the framework on which supervisors can evaluate and put into perspective the employee suggestions to which they are subjected, and hence serves to increase their feelings of competence, self-confidence, and autonomy. With this insight, administrators can better make decisions about work duties, organizational policies, and management choices. Once these issues are addressed comprehensively and maintained on a regular basis, the working environment and the job itself should improve. (Refer to Figure 2).

Figure 2: Maslow's Hierarchy of Needs theory and Herzberg's Motivation Hygiene theory combined.

MOTIVATION

Self – Realization Needs (Relate to Maslow)	**Job Related Satisfiers (Relate to Herzberg)**
Reaching your potential	Involvement in planning
Independence	Related to work itself
Creativity	Freedom to make decisions
Self Expression	Creative work to perform
	Opportunities for development
Esteem Needs	**Job-Related Satisfiers**
Responsibility	Status Symbols
Self Respect	Merit Awards
Recognition	Challenging Work
Sense of Accomplishment	Sharing in Decisions
Sense of Competence	Opportunity for Advancement

MAINTENANCE

Social Needs	**Job Related Satisfiers**
Companionship	*Interaction with others*
Acceptance	*Team Spirit*
Love and Affection	*Friendly Co-Workers*
Group Membership	
Safety Needs	***Job-Related Satisfiers***
Security of Self and Possessions	*Safe Working Conditions*
Avoidance of Risks	*Seniority*
Avoidance of Harm	*Fringe Benefits*
Avoidance of Pain	*Proper Supervision*
	Sound company policies, programs
Physical Needs	***Job-Related Satisfiers***
Food	*Pleasant Working Conditions*
Clothing	*Adequate Wage or Salary*
Shelter	*Rest Period*
Comfort	*Labor-Saving Devices*
Self-Preservation	*Efficient Work Methods*

Source: Herzberg, F., Mausner, B., & Snyderman, B. B. (1959). *The Motivation to Work* (2nd ed.). New York: John Wiley & Sons; Maslow, A. H. (1970). *Motivation and Personality* (2nd ed.). New York: Harper and Row.

The existing literature on organizational theory suggests that motivation factors cannot be *effectively* addressed unless maintenance factors are first addressed. Existing literature suggests that workers rate motivation factors such as recognition, achievement, growth, responsibility, advancement and status as a priority over all other categories. Yet maintenance needs, when satisfied, tend to minimize dissatisfaction while doing little to motivate an individual to higher levels of performance. because satisfaction of the motivating factors permits the individual to grow, develop, and increase their ability to perform, it is suggested that it is necessary to address maintenance factors within the organization first before you can effectively motivate your employees.

Sociology References:

Scientific Management: A systematic attempt to analyze work in order to identify the most efficient way to accomplish a given task. F.W. Taylor likened the human body to a machine and conducted time and motion studies to determine the most efficient way to make use of it.

The Hawthorne Effect: Researchers at the Western Electric Company monitored by researchers discovered that the level of attention (i.e., recognition) paid to the employees increased production levels.

Communication Structure: A communication structure is the pattern of interactions revealing who communicates with whom, how often, and for how long as it exists in every social system.

Social Structure: Every social system has a structure. The structure of a social system can be analyzed in terms of two characteristics, relationships and distributions. The *relationships* in a system connect its various parts to one another and, hence, to the *system as a whole.* The parts can range from the statuses people occupy to entire systems such as groups, organizations, communities, and societies.

Formal Organization: A formal organization is a social system organized around specific goals and usually consisting of several interrelated groups or subsystems. Formal organizations are governed by clearly stated, rigidly enforced norms.

Works Cited

Herzberg, F., B. F. Mausner, and B. B. Snyderman, 1959. *The Motivation to Work* 2nd ed.. New York: John Wiley & Sons: Maslow, A. H. (1970). *Motivation and Personality* 2nd ed. New York: Harper and Row.

Notes

1.   It is important to indicate that Watkins swept in on a Democratic tide in the 2007 election, along with more than 40 judges. Watkins realized the demographic change when he first ran for office in 2002. The political and demographic changes in this election process are examples of changes occurring in the organizational environment of which changed the mission of the organization.

STEP 13

IMPROVE THE JUSTICE ADMINISTRATION PROCESS THROUGH EFFECTIVE PROGRAMS

In order to improve the criminal justice system, you must select programs that will have a positive impact on the effective administration of justice; for this guide a community justice concept is used as an example. The following is an overview of a position paper by Alan Rosenthal and Elaine Wolf entitled Unlocking the Potential of Reentry and Reintegration-A Reintegrative Sentencing Model (October 2004)[1]. It addresses reintegration as the goal that is used as a model and basis for the development of a community justice program that significantly changes the mission and goals of the criminal justice system.

Rosenthal and Wolf explain the purpose of this reintegration model by describe a new approach to reentry practice and policy in the context of the processing of a criminal case. They view reentry planning as ideally being incorporated into activities taking place at six points during the pendency of a criminal case and service of a sentence: decision making regarding pretrial release; plea bargaining and sentence negotiations; sentencing; jail and prison programming; the provision of supportive services at the time of release; and decision making regarding parole revocation. If such planning were systematically incorporated into these six phases of criminal case processing, people involved in the criminal justice system would be more likely to reintegrate into their communities successfully and maximize their capacity for productive citizenship. This approach to reentry planning is consistent with the perspective of the Center for Community Alternatives (CCA), a community-based organization whose principal mission is to reduce society's reliance on incarceration. CCA views its refinement of conceptualizing the reentry process as being integral to its mission and a natural outgrowth of its direct service programs and research activities. Specific examples of its experience are sentencing advocacy services to defense attorneys (Client Specific Planning); outpatient drug treatment services to court-mandated women (Crossroads); employment and HIV-related services to reentering inmates; aftercare services for people in recovery who have a history of involvement in the criminal justice system (Syracuse Recovery Community Support Program); trainings for reentering people and for defense attorneys; and evaluations of reentry programs.

Rosenthal and Wolf describe their vision of reentry planning as a six-stage approach, clarify how it differs from the traditional reentry planning model, and explain the advantages of this approach. To unlock the potential of reentry, Rosenthal and Wolf propose transforming traditional sentencing by *incorporating reintegration* into the American sentencing model. This is accomplished by adding it to the four traditional goals of sentencing; incapacitation, deterrence, punishment, and rehabilitation. [2]

Reentry and Reintegration

The growing number of people released from prison,,650,000 each year, according to the Bureau of Justice Statistics (Hughes and Wilson 2003)(Bureau of Justice Statistics (2002), has caused a surge of empirical and conceptual work in the area of reentry. Rosenthal and Wolf suggest that recent work has emerged a view of reentry that defines reentry as the process and experience of leaving prison after serving a sentence and returning to society; this includes the activities and programming conducted to prepare prisoners to return safely to the community and to reintegrate as law-abiding citizens. The related concept known as reintegration is the process by which the reentering former prisoners adjust and reconnect to employment, families, communities, and civic life. Current reentry models focus on providing reentry services to people immediately upon their release from service of the incarcerative portion of the sentence. More advanced models recognize the need to prepare for the transition back to the community prior to release from incarceration and envision that reentry planning begins when the person enters prison. Although the reentry planning differs between these two models, the definition of reentry remains the same in both models. Rosenthal and Wolf suggest that reentry be defined as a six-stage process that begins at arrest and ends at parole: This process is described below.

The Six-Stage Reentry Model

There are many issues associated with reentry as early as the time of arrest. A sentencing advocate working with a defense attorney can identify these challenges and develop plans to address them. Reentry planning can be incorporated into advocacy and specific reentry activities at several different phases of the criminal case. A working paper by Alan Rosenthal and Elaine Wolf entitled Unlocking the Potential of Reentry and Reintegration-A Reintegrative Sentencing Model (October 2004)[1] lists six stages or points at which reentry planning can be effectively used for both advocacy and successful reintegration:

1. Pretrial release
2. Plea bargaining and sentence negotiations
3. Sentencing
4. Self-development and preparation for reentry while in prison

5. Release after serving sentence

6. Parole revocation

Reentry planning is described to begin at the time of the arrest as a plan is constructed to support the advocacy for pretrial release. Reentry planning at any of the six stages of the criminal justice process can either lead to reentry or to the next stage where the reentry plan is again used.

Rosenthal and Wolf's Reasons for a Six-Stage Approach

Reentry planning that commences at the pretrial stage offers several advantages from the perspective of professional practice standards for defense counsel, fiscal responsibility, efficiency, public safety, and social justice. It serves as a catalyst for defense counsel to fulfill his or her professional responsibilities to address early diversion, develop a plan for meeting the needs of the accused and a program for rehabilitation, and develop information that would support a sentence other than incarceration. Additionally reentry planning:

• reduces the use of prison, which is both costly and criminogenic;

• increases the likelihood of successful reintegration, thus promoting public safety;

• expedites and facilitates the systematic referral of people in need of services;

• promotes rational, less punitive, individualized sentences; and

• promotes efficiency and consistency of planning for reentry.

Rosenthal and Wolf Reintegration-Focused Sentencing Model
Reintegration as a Sentencing Goal

Rosenthal and Wolf explain that the focus on reentry over the last few years, culminating when President George W. Bush's highlighted the issue in his 2004 State of the Union Address, should be seen as an opportunity. It is an opportunity to reconsider the traditional goals of sentencing, which include incapacitation, deterrence, punishment, and rehabilitation. During the past 30 years, as we have filled our old prisons, and built many new ones, the goal of rehabilitation has been all but abandoned, leaving us with little more than punitive sentencing practices (Garland 2001). *Reintegration should supersede the much criticized goal of rehabilitation.* Reintegration as a sentencing goal changes the focus from "fixing the offender" to a more complex recognition of shared responsibility.

Rosenthal and Wolf further explain that in U.S. Supreme Court Justice Anthony Kennedy's address to the American Bar Association on August 9, 2003, (Kennedy 2003), Kennedy called for fundamental changes in current judicial and corrections practices. He implored the American Bar Association to initiate a public discussion about punishment and sentencing: "When it costs so much more to incarcerate a prisoner than to educate a child, we should take special care to ensure that we are not incarcerating too many persons for too long. It requires one with more expertise in the area than I possess to offer a complete analysis, but it does seem justified to say this: Our resources are misspent, our punishments too severe, our sentences too long." Justice Kennedy went on to underscore the need for changes in sentencing practices, perhaps foreshadowing the development of a sentencing model that incorporates reintegration as a sentencing goal. "The debate over the goals of sentencing is a difficult one, but we should not cease to conduct it. Prevention and incapacitation are often legitimate goals. There are realistic limits to efforts at rehabilitation. We must try, however, to bridge the gap between proper skepticism about rehabilitation on the one hand and improper refusal to acknowledge that the more than two million inmates in the United States are human beings whose minds and spirits we must try to reach." (Kennedy 2003).

The literature suggests that a reintegration-focused sentencing model would bridge that gap. This literature further suggests that the opportunity to reconsider sentencing philosophy is provided not only by the emergence of reentry as a public policy issue and an awakening to the severity of mandatory sentences, but by the emerging theories of *community justice.* Making reintegration the primary sentencing goal is consistent with the theories of community justice explored by Karp and Clear (2000). Community justice, as they conceptualize it, has twin foci: restoration and reintegration. Public safety and the quality of community life are promoted by the restoration of the community and the victim and also by the effective reintegration of offenders. At the same time, community justice places punishment as a sanctioning philosophy in a greatly diminished role (Karp and Clear 2000).

Rosenthal and Wolf (2004) describe reintegration at the center of a reintegration-focused model by returning the defendant back to the community in a way that promotes public safety. They suggest that the four traditional goals of sentencing recognized as incapacitation, deterrence, rehabilitation, and punishment should remain but are all considered in the context of reintegration. Placing the goal of reintegration within the range of goals to be served by sentencing will bring us back to a more individualized approach. It will require each judge, at the time of sentencing, to address several questions. "How will this sentence promote the ability of this defendant to reenter society successfully at the end of her incarceration?" "Will a community-based sentence better serve the end of reintegration?" "How can we best promote public safety now and in the future with a reintegration plan for this defendant?"

On June 7, 2006, Governor George Pataki signed into law an important modification affecting sentencing in New York. Penal Law §1.05(6) has been amended to add a new goal to the traditional sentencing model that includes deterrence, rehabilitation, retribution, and incapacitation: the promotion of the defendant's successful and productive reentry and reintegration into society (Chapter 98 of the Laws of 2006). This amendment to New York's Penal Law became effective immediately, and marks a significant shift by the legislature in sentencing policy. The new law will require every judge presiding at sentencing in a criminal case to consider carefully the extent to which any given sentence will help promote the convicted person's reintegration into society. Under the amended law a new and increased significance is placed on breaking the cycle of recidivism by imposing sentences of a length and type that will promote successful reintegration and increase public safety. [3]

Sociology References:

Social Control: A concept that refers to the ways in which peoples thoughts, feelings, appearance, and behavior are regulated in social systems. Control may be exerted through various forms of coercion such as the authority of the criminal justice system. *Coercion, however, is generally ineffective* as the sole means of social control. *Far more important is socialization,* through which people come to identify with the social system and its values and norms and acquire a stake in maintaining these as well as their sense of belonging to the system. Fear of ridicule or exclusion is a powerful inducement to conform as well as the risk of being shamed.

Works Cited

Bureau of Justice Statistics. 2002. "Reentry Trends in the U.S. Federal Supervised Release." Washington, D.C.: Bureau of Justice Statistics, U.S. Department of Justice.

Garland, David. 2001. The Culture of Control: Crime and Social Order in Contemporary Society. Chicago: The University of Chicago Press.

Hughes, Timothy and Doris James Wilson. 2003, "Reentry Trends in the United States" Washington, D.C.: Bureau of Justice Statistics, U.S. Department of Justice.

Karp, David R. and Todd R. Clear. 2000. "Community Justice'; a Conceptual framework." *Boundary Changes in Criminal Justice Organizations* pp. 323-368Washington, D.C.: National Institute of Justice.

Kennedy, Anthony M. 2003. Address at the American Bar Association Annual Meeting, August 9, 2003. http://www.supremecourtus.gov/publicinfo/speeches/sp_08-09-03.html.

Rosenthal, Alan and Elaine Wolf. 2004. *Unlocking the Potential of Reentry and Reintegration - A Reintegrative Sentencing Model* [A Working Paper] New York Center for Community Alternative Justice Strategies. **http://www.communityalternatives.org/pdfs/unlocking_potential.pdf**

Travis, Jeremy. 2001. "Heretical Propositions for Improving Re-Entry." Comments at Roundtable on Constructing and Coping With Incarceration and Family Re-Entry: Perspectives from the Field, November 15-16, 2001. Philadelphia, PA: National Center on Fathers and Families, University of Pennsylvania.

Notes

1.   This reintegrative sentencing model was championed by the *Interfaith Coalition of Advocates for Reentry and Employment (ICARE),* an alliance of communities of faith, direct service providers, and policy organizations including the New York State Council of Churches, Legal Action Center, Center for Community Alternatives, Reentry Net/NY, and many congregations throughout New York State.

2.   The four traditional goals of sentencing should remain (incapacitation, deterrence, punishment, and rehabilitation) but are all considered in the context of reintegration.

3.   **The HTML or Word version of this   Bill** can be found at **http://www.communityalternatives.org/articles/bill%20text.htm**

13A-13H

EXAMPLES OF PROGRAMS THAT POSITIVELY IMPACT THE CRIMINAL JUSTICE SYSTEM'S TOTAL SYSTEM OUTCOMES

STEP 13-A

Community Justice and Reentry Advisory Programs [1]

Community justice is a broad strategy that is based on three principles. First, community justice selects high-impact locations where there is a concentration of crime and criminal justice activities, in order to develop special strategies designed to improve the quality of community life, especially by promoting public safety. Second, community justice approaches its tasks in these areas by working to strengthen the capacity of informal systems of social control, such as families, neighborhood groups, friends, and social supports. Third, in order to strengthen community capacity, community justice initiatives develop partnerships with residents, businesses, and other social services to coordinate the way public safety problems are addressed. It is possible for you to implement a community justice strategy within the traditional criminal justice functions of law enforcement, courts, and corrections.

For police, community justice involves interacting with community institutions and representatives to tailor police and community activities to the various problems residents perceive to be undermining their quality of life.

Community justice for prosecution and courts requires that prosecutors, defense attorneys, and judges become familiar with the various public-safety problems that come to the attention of the courts. Special legal approaches can be developed to target problems specific to particular communities.

Regarding community justice in corrections, the focus has been on the use of probation, parole, and other *community-based* correctional programs for offenders. In such corrections endeavors, offenders are not only supervised and served in the community, but also draw upon community resources [2] in order to encourage the development of positive behaviors and lifestyles for offenders (Clear et. al., 2003). Therefore, it is suggested to establish a local community-based reentry council advisory group that consists of individuals and/or organizations throughout the community to address the development of a planning strategy for the effective reintegration of ex-offenders, with the goal of reducing recidivism, supporting victims and promoting community safety. A local reentry council is an advisory board structured to facilitate the collaboration of community groups, public health officials, treatment providers, educational institutions, legislators, human services groups, housing officials, workforce development groups, faith based organizations, families, former inmates, victims' advocates, law enforcement agencies, prosecutors, courts and correctional agencies, in order to develop a resource planning strategy for the effective reintegration of ex-offenders.

The Council of State Governments (CSG) **http://www.csg.org/** established a Re-Entry Policy Council (RPC) in 2001 to develop recommendations to improve the likelihood that adults released from prison and jail will avoid crime and become productive, healthy members of families and communities. To guide the work of the RPC in the areas of public safety and restorative activities, supportive health and housing, and workforce development and employment opportunities, CSG partnered with 10 organizations:

- American Probation and Parole Association **http://www.appa-net.org/**
- Reentry Policy Council: **http://www.reentrypolicy.org/reentry/default.aspx**
- Reentry Policy Council Guide: **http://www.reentrypolicy.org/reentry/SA_Introduction.aspx**
- Association of State Correctional Administrators: **http://www.asca.net/**
- Corporation for Supportive Housing: **http://www.csh.org/**
- National Association of Housing and Redevelopment Officials: **http://www.nahro.org/index.cfm**
- National Association of State Alcohol/Drug Abuse Directors: **http://www.nasadad.org/**
- National Association of State Mental Health Program Directors: **http://www.nawb.org/**
- National Association of Workforce Boards: **http://www.nawb.org/forum2006/schedule.htm**
- National Center for State Courts: **http://www.ncsconline.org/**
- Police Executive Research Forum: **http://www.policeforum.org/**
- Urban Institute: **http://www.urban.org/**

Sociological References:

Social Problem: A social problem can best be described by looking at the term in two parts: the problem and what makes it social. For a problem to be social it must involve a social system and must be *caused by underlying social conditions*. For example, drug abuse is a social problem because it is rooted in social conditions that make it possible and promote it. This includes the availability of drugs as part of the material cultural and the widespread cultural promotion of general drug use from aspirin to alcohol, as a legitimate and effective response to personal and social conditions such as disease, poverty, and social alienation.

Works Cited

Clear, Todd R. Eric Cadora, Sarah Bryer, Charles Swartz 2003 *Community Justice.* NCJ Number 196696. Belmont, CA Wadsworth Publishing Co.

Notes

1. The Community Justice concept is a strategy that many criminal justice pundits consider to be the criminal justice reform model. See Figure 7 for a description of the Community Justice Model.

2. A reintegration council may serve as the group that can provide these additional resources. More information on reentry councils can be found in Step 13 F.

STEP 13-B

Police Programs

The police, mission, goals and objectives will be discussed and compared to the criminal justice system. It will be argued that "programs" such as problem oriented approaches to policing can be more effective at improving the overall justice system mission. The traditional bureaucratic and reform models of policing are debated along with other major findings such as community and problem oriented policing. In order to meet the goals of community justice it is important for you to consider redefining the mission of the police organization with a focus on minimizing the reliance on traditional law enforcement practices and becoming more community-based.

David Carter, Ph.D., of Michigan State University explains on his Web site, **http://www.cj.msu.edu/~people/cp/cpmeasure.html,** that community policing appears inconsistent with traditional era police management. Community policing seems most compatible with contemporary management philosophies such as total quality management (TQM), value-added management, and the re-engineering the corporation approach. Community policing shares with these management systems an emphasis on customer demand, providing the best possible service, *comprehensive problem solving, and employee motivation and job satisfaction.* Based on contemporary management principles, a number of improvements in police departments have been suggested it order to support a more community-based approached to policing. Dr. Carter reiterates the following points, as previously explained by (Couper and Lobitz in1993):

- The police executive life and leadership style should be in tune with community expectations.
- Police executives must listen to both employees and community members and provide ongoing feedback.
- Personnel recruitment and selection should be future directed and geared toward fulfilling the departmental vision.
- Policing should primarily focus on neighborhood and citizen problems, not on time management and officer deployment schemes.
- Community perceptions of crime, police performance, and quality of life problems are significant and should not be ignored.
- Police executives should strive to provide the best possible service and value to the community in relation to police resources expenditures.

Carter suggests that these changes will not come easily, but experience suggests that a transition pattern often develops. At first, traditional police approaches are recognized as limited or even unsuccessful. Second, attitudes among administrators, line personnel, and citizens begin to change. Third, community assessments are performed and police responsibilities redefined. Fourth, new operational and organizational approaches are developed. Fifth, the community is enlisted to work cooperatively with the police. Finally, both law enforcement and the community will benefit from the *care* taken with this holistic approach to policing.

Community policing demands that *personal qualifications and education of police officers be raised.* Community policing demands that officers be suited by personal characteristics and education to earn the trust of the community as well as their own confidence in their ability to perform this new approach to policing. For example, a police performance review, under a community-based policing program, may include categories such as: ability to engage in interagency networking, problem solving, mediation, negotiation, community organization, and many other categories that do not currently appear on a police officer evaluation. Although making arrests and maintaining general order are obviously essential, input from the community becomes a primary source of guidance and direction (Hahn 1998, pp. 90-93). Hahn explains that raised self-esteem is one of the first fruits of higher education and those who "feel good about themselves" are always prepared to relate to those with different opinions and diverse lifestyles (pp.91). Therefore, the challenge of community policing is finding ways to make *quality and quantity* accountable commodities. This means that the police officer must be engaged in the community and organizational activities and be responsible for the end/measurable results.

Because community policing focuses on neighborhood and citizen problems, George Kelling (2004), co-author of "Broken Windows," suggests that since the U.S. announced its war on terrorism, police are facing a new challenges and that problem solving strategies associated with community policing can effectively address this mandate: While it has been a challenge to define the new responsibilities and relationships that should occur between federal agencies, there has been much less attention paid to the role that police must play in homeland security and protecting critical national infrastructure. This is unfortunate, because terrorism's equivalent to fare jumping in the New York City subways are illegal border crossings, forged documents, and other relatively *minor crimes* that terrorists use to fund their operations. Disgruntled workers, ex-offenders, students suspended from school or demonstrating an issue, and many other organizations and individuals that support different causes can all be a source of violent or terrorists incidents in our small communities as well as the larger cities.

Police can work closer with the community and social service organizations to prevent terrorism by identifying the aforementioned issues. They can also

pinpoint certain experiences and events in a person's life that may cause them to become radical, to the extent of turning to violence to resolve perceived grievances. Addressing these issues proactively with the community is critical to understanding how terrorist groups recruit new members and sustain support for their activities within local communities. For example, in the United Kingdom, social justice issues impact the Muslim, communities resulting in high levels of disadvantage. Work has been underway for some time on addressing the inequalities they experience. The Government's broader race and community cohesion strategy, titled *Improving Opportunities, Strengthening Society* (IOSS) published in January 2005) outlined a cross-government response to reducing inequalities, particularly those associated with race and faith, and to increasing community cohesion. In particular, the strategy includes actions being taken to help Muslims improve their educational performance, employment opportunities, and housing conditions (MI5 2006). More information on this approach can be found at the follow Web site:
http://www.homeoffice.gov.uk/documents/improving-opportunity-stratwas

Sociology Reference:

Social Order: A social cohesion through which systems are held together. It is sometimes synonymous with social control and other methods used to ensure that people obey norms and support values.

Works Cited

Couper D. and H. Lobitz. 1993. "Leadership for Change: A National Agenda". *The Police Chief*, 60(12), 15-19. Cox, D. R. (1972).

Hahn, P.H. 1998 *Emerging Trends in Criminal Justice*, pp.90-93.Thousand Oaks, California, Sage Publications

Kelling, George (2004) *Hard Won Lessons: How Police Fight Terrorism the United Kingdom* " Introduction: Do Police Matter." P.1-4. Manhattan Institute for Policy Research, New York, New York.

MI5, The Security Service "Preventing terrorism by countering the radicalisation of individuals" *Countering International Terrorism: The United Kingdom's Strategy* July 2006 **http://www.mi5.gov.uk/output/Page555.html**

STEP 13 C

Prosecution

The prosecutor's mission, goals, and objectives will be discussed and compared to the criminal justice system. It will be argued that "programs" such as Community-Based Prosecution are problem oriented approaches that prosecutors can use in conjunction with policing and can be more effective at improving the overall justice system mission. It is suggested that you re-define the mission of prosecution and focus on the need to minimize the reliance on traditional practices, become more community based, decentralize operations, and improve relationships with the police and community. A community-based and problem oriented approach to prosecution and defense is suggested and is paramount for the offender reintegration process.

Community-based prosecution involves a long-term, proactive partnership among the prosecutor's office, law enforcement, the community, and public and private organizations, whereby the authority of the prosecutor's office is used to solve problems, improve public safety, and enhance the quality of life of community members. According to the National Research Council (2001), "the most universal ingredient" of community prosecution is the addition of crime *prevention* to the prosecutor's mission. Under this emerging philosophy, prosecutors are viewed not just as officers of the court who come on scene once a crime has occurred, but rather as members of the community who have the power to stop crime from occurring. This community-oriented prosecution has become not just a new program, but a new strategy for prosecutors. Community prosecutors use tools such as nuisance abatement, drug-free and prostitute-free zones, restorative justice, community courts, gun reduction programs, truancy abatement, and graffiti cleanup to improve neighborhood safety.

Community prosecution has progressed significantly since its inception in the early 1990s. As recently as 1995, approximately six jurisdictions throughout the United States engaged in community prosecution, and then only in urban settings. Community prosecution continues to evolve and to spread beyond metropolitan cities to rural, small, and tribal jurisdictions. An APRI survey conducted in 2000 revealed that 49 percent of prosecutors' offices practice community prosecution in some form (**Nugent and Rainville 2001**). According to the *Bureau of Justice Statistics Bulletin* (July 2002), during 2001, 68% percent of all prosecutors' offices used tools other than traditional criminal prosecution to address community problems. City attorneys' offices are also beginning to see and believe in the value of working with law enforcement and the community to develop creative solutions to livability issues.

The American Prosecutors Research Institute (APRI) further clarifies that creative solutions developed by prosecutors around the country range from minor changes in how their organizations prioritize cases, to leading the way in redefining the role of the prosecutor. Prosecutors are becoming partnership builders and bringing the police, the community, and other criminal justice and local agencies together to find ways they can work together to solve livability issues in neighborhoods. All share the tenet of community prosecution first identified by APRI in 1995, prosecutors transcending their traditional roles as case processors and forging partnerships with law enforcement, the community, and various public and private agencies to act as problem solvers. Community prosecution is a grassroots approach to law enforcement. It involves traditional and non-traditional initiatives to work within a community to prevent crime, thus reducing the number of arrests and prosecutions.

In late 1990, Multnomah County, Oregon's district attorney assigned a senior deputy to work for one year on a neighborhood-based prosecution project in one of Portland's inner-city districts. This idea of a special prosecutor caught on, and other Neighborhood District Attorneys (NDAs) were formed. The NDAs were effective in creating two-way communication to link themselves to both citizens and police officers (Boland 1996). Neighborhood defense teams also represented individuals accused of crimes who could not afford private lawyers and were based in the community. Instead of waiting for the court to assign legal representation to the client, the defense teams encouraged residents to call the office any time and the client was represented by the entire legal team, which contrasts with the usual practice of assigning a client to a single attorney (Stone 1996).

The literature suggests that the results of programs of this type disclose a more just and comprehensive approach to addressing crime and criminal behavior. This approach not only benefits targeting the individual problem defendants and the events leading to the development of criminal cases also but the needed legal defense services and representation that were neglected.

Sociology Reference:

Social Order: A social cohesion through which systems are held together. It is sometimes synonymous with social control and other methods used to ensure that people obey norms and support values.

Works Cited

Boland, B. 1996. "What is Community Prosecution?" *National Institute of Justice Journal,* Issue: 231, August: 35-40.

National Research Council 2001. "What's Changing in Prosecution? Report of a Workshop." Committee on Law and Justice, Phillip Heymann and Carol Petrie, Editors. Division of Behavioral and Social Sciences and Education. Washington, DC: National Academy Press.

Nugent, M.E. and G. A. Rainville 2001. "The State of Community Prosecution: Results of a National Survey." *The Prosecutor.* 13(2): 26-33. Alexandria, VA: National District Attorneys' Association.

Stone, Christopher. 1996 "Community Defense and the Challenge of Community Justice", *National Institute of Justice Journal* Issue 231, August. 41-45.

STEP 13-D

Court Programs

The court's mission, goals, and objectives are discussed and compared to the criminal justice system. It is debated that the effective administration of punishment is the element of justice that is needed to reform the criminal justice system along with programs such as community courts, reentry councils, and courts as the vehicles that will implement these changes. The mission of the courts must be changed in order for them to become more community based. In order to achieve this goal, two types of courts are suggested:

Reentry Courts

The Office of Juvenile Justice and Delinquency Prevention (OJJDP) Model Programs Guide [1] explains that reentry courts are specialized courts that help reduce recidivism and improve public safety through the use of judicial oversight. The responsibilities generally assigned to reentry courts include: (1) review offenders' reentry progress and problems; (2) order offenders to participate in various treatment and reintegration programs; (3) use drug and alcohol testing and other checks to monitor compliance; (4) apply graduated sanctions to offenders who do not comply with treatment requirements; (5) provide modest incentive rewards for sustained clean drug tests and other positive behaviors. See this Web page for an explanation of the characteristics of a reentry court: **http://www.ncjrs.gov/pdffiles1/ojp/sl000389.pdf**
http://www.lhc.ca.gov/lhcdir/womenparole/SurbeckMay04.pdf

The traditional responsibility of the court to an offender ends when a defendant is sentenced by a judge. Judges typically have no role in the broad array of activities that carry out the terms of the sentence, the preparation of the offender for release, or the transition of the offender back into the community. Nevertheless, a combination of trends in sentencing, incarceration, and post-release supervision is affording the opportunity for courts to become the principal force behind these activities. For instance, widely recognized increases in incarceration rates over the past 20 years have led to record numbers of prisoners. Accompanying the increases in incarceration are increases in the amount of time served, primarily due to truth-in-sentencing laws and the shift away from discretionary release. Despite more prisoners being incarcerated and serving longer sentences, the availability of treatment programs in prisons is questionable, and program participation among prisoners has been declining over the past decade (Lynch and Sabol 2001). Finally, the emphasis on supervision over treatment is also evident outside of correctional institutions, with post-release supervision officers facing increasingly higher caseloads yet lower per capita spending (Petersilia 1999).

Although the organization structures of these courts vary, partnerships of this type normally require judicial involvement and supervision of the offender throughout the entire sentence and re-entry process, thus establishing a more comprehensive approach to criminal justice. These judge-centered models feature an ongoing central role for the judge, a commitment between the court and offender and judicial discretion within the sentencing process (U.S. Department of Justice: 1999, pp. 2-8). The literature suggests that improvements of this type will provide a more individualized approach to the justice process and improve the offender reintegration process.

Sociology Reference:

Justice: A concept referring to fairness and to the process of people getting what they deserve. In a legal sense, justice consists of treating everyone according to the law, of guaranteeing civil rights, and following prescribed procedures in a consistent manner.

Works Cited

Lynch, James P. and William J. Sabol. 2001. *Prisoner Reentry in Perspective.* Washington, D.C.: Urban Institute, Justice Policy.

Petersilia, J. 1999. "Parole and Prisoner Reentry in the United States," Prisons: *Crime and Justice.* Michael Tonry and Joan Petersilia. The University of Chicago Press.

U. S. Department of Justice, Office of Justice Programs, *Key Elements of Successful Adjudication Partnerships* May 1999) [On-Line serial] Bureau of Justice Assistance NCJ 173949, 1-11.

Notes

1. Model Programs Guide Version 2.5; The OJJDP Model Programs Guide was created and developed by Development Services Group under Cooperative Agreement #2004-JF-FX-K101. **http://www.dsgonline.com/mpg2.5/mpg_index.htm**

STEP 13-E

Community Courts

The Center for Court Innovation (CCI) is an independent research and development arm in New York that functions as the court system's independent research and development group, creating demonstration projects that test new ideas. The Center's projects include:

- community courts
- drug courts
- reentry courts
- domestic violence courts
- mental health courts

The CCI provides an overview of community courts in operation across the United States:

The first community court opened in midtown Manhattan in 1993. Focusing on quality-of-life offenses (drug possession, shoplifting, vandalism, prostitution, and the like), the Midtown Community Court combined punishment and help, sentencing low-level offenders to perform visible community restitution and receive on-site social services, including drug treatment, counseling, and job training. The community courts that have followed in the Midtown Court's wake seek to achieve many goals, such as reduced crime, increased engagement between citizens and the courts, improved perceptions of neighborhood safety, and a greater level of accountability for low-level, "quality-of-life" offenders.

As yet, no consensus has emerged regarding how to best measure the goals of these programs, primarily due to the large variety of models adopted by different courts. To date, there are seven notable community court evaluations focusing on four community courts: Midtown Community Court, Red Hook Community Justice Center in Brooklyn; New York; Hennepin County Community Court in Minneapolis, Minnesota; and Hartford Community Court in Connecticut. CCI summarizes the basic findings from these evaluations:

1. The Midtown study is the only one to tackle the impact on crime in the community, documenting encouraging results: Prostitution arrests were down 56 percent and illegal vending arrests were down 24 percent following the opening of the community court. Data from ethnographic observations and individual interviews confirmed this drop in criminal activity. In addition, defendants who had completed at least 90 days of court-mandated drug treatment demonstrated a reduction in annual arrest rates over three years compared to prior to the Midtown intervention (2.3 annual arrests pre-Midtown versus 0.9 post-Midtown).

2. The 2000 Hennepin study includes a comprehensive cost-benefit analysis. Overall, the community court was found to be more expensive than regular case processing, costing an additional net $704.52 per case, but the authors noted that there are many additional benefits that cannot be quantified in monetary value to offset the costs. The only benefit that was included is the value of community service performed by defendants. Other benefits included the improved quality of life in the neighborhood and the improved quality and efficiency of decision-making due to increased information sharing.

3. The Midtown study includes a cost-benefit analysis as well, but that analysis is, by the authors' own admission, limited due to lack of ability to quantify fully all benefits and costs. What the Midtown study did find, though, are significant monetary benefits to the court system—including approximately $100,000 in reduced costs due to decreased pre-arraignment detention, $500,000 in reduced costs due to reduced use of jail, $570,000 in future reduced costs due to reduced prostitution arrests, and $150,000 in benefits derived from the community service of defendants for a total of approximately $1.3 million annually.

4. The Hartford study included interviews with offenders to document their perceptions of their experience. Overall, offenders thought the community court was a good idea (96 percent), that their sentence was *fair* (73 percent), that the community court was helping Hartford neighborhoods (83 percent), and that all people were treated fairly at the community court (61 percent). Similarly, the Red Hook community survey (Moore 2004) found that the majority (56 percent) of those who had had a case at the Justice Center reported a positive experience. The Hartford offenders also thought the prosecutor was fair (76 percent) and an overwhelming majority (91 percent) thought they were treated with respect by the judge. As is typical in Connecticut for misdemeanor cases, most defendants had no legal representation (79 percent). Many thought they needed a lawyer (84 percent).

5. The Midtown study included interviews with female prostitutes who had been arrested and brought to the Midtown Community Court. These women had both positive and negative comments about the Court. On the positive side, they commented that, compared to the traditional downtown court, the community court processed their cases quicker, the holding cells were cleaner, the food was better, and the staff more sympathetic. On the other hand, the women com-

plained that the alternative sentences at Midtown made it more difficult for them to "work"; furthermore, many women mentioned that they would continue to engage in prostitution, but would move out of the Midtown catchment area. (In response the Midtown Community Court made several efforts to combat the potential "displacement effect." Most notably, the Court now handles all prostitution arrests in Manhattan.)

6. The 2000 Hennepin study included focus groups and interviews with stakeholders of the community court, including staff and treatment providers. The treatment providers in particular were pleased with the court's linking offenders to services, holding them accountable, and locating key service providers in the same building.

7. In Hartford, staff felt that reacting strongly to quality-of-life crimes prevents future offenses because offenders know these actions are going to be taken seriously. Similar to Hennepin, Hartford staff liked the balance between punishment and help and thought accountability was important. Overall, Hartford staff thought the community court provides an "opportunity for a second chance" with "a client-centered" social service delivery system. The Hartford study also included interviews with staff that documented the implementation challenges and barriers in opening an innovative program within the criminal justice system.

The CCI explains that as the community court models spread across the country, it is important for the evaluation literature to catch up. There are several methodologies highlighted here, but, to date, no one single study has covered all aspects of evaluation process evaluation, outcome evaluation, community impact survey, offender perceptions, and cost-benefit analysis. The Midtown and Hennepin evaluations come the closest but are now several years old. Future analysis should seek to give a more comprehensive picture of these complex projects.

Works Cited

The Center for Court Innovation 2004: February. [On-Line Serial]: New York, NY. **http://www.courtinnovation.org/index.cfm**

STEP 13-F

Corrections

The correctional system mission and goals are discussed and compared to the mission and goals of the criminal justice system. The concepts of punishments are discussed along with how the corrections administrator must deal with the variety of offenders with the responsibilities of rehabilitation, incarceration, and reintegration. An integrated justice model is introduced that is deemed an effective strategy for correctional reform.

Community Corrections

The mission of community corrections must be changed to reflect a new commitment to providing services through an *evidence-based practice approach,* which is structured to meet the crminogenic needs of individual offenders through empirically based "what works" research in order to assist in the rehabilitation and reintegration process.

State legislatures should pass laws that establish local community transition programs. The statutes will allow each county in the state to develop their own reintegration transition programs, to which the inmates of the state prison and jail systems may be released early to community supervision and corrections departments. The law should permit county judges to determine what level of supervision would be utilized for each offender (serious crimes will be excluded from consideration). This process will either support or fill in the gap in existing state parole practices. Additionally, it is suggested to link these transition programs to a voluntary reentry court program. The reentry court program should supervise the offenders for a designated number of months, and within the first four to six months, of their release they should be placed under electronic monitoring while also receiving direct access to assistance with issues they face as returning offenders (housing, job training, etc.). The mission of the project is to significantly lower the rate of recidivism of returning offenders through gradually decreasing levels of supervision and enhanced delivery of services, while, at the same time, maintaining public safety.

Reintegration Councils

Reentry councils should be structured to facilitate the collaboration of community groups, public health officials, treatment providers, educational institutions, legislators, human services groups, housing officials, workforce development groups, faith based organizations, families, former inmates, victims' advocates, law enforcement agencies, prosecutors, courts, and correctional agencies to develop a planning strategy for the effective reintegration of ex-offenders, thereby reducing recidivism, supporting victims, and promoting public safety.

The goal of a Reentry Council is to develop a comprehensive reentry strategic plan based on evaluation and assessed needs of the categories below:

• Linking offenders to sustainable employment through effective training, education, and employer development, thereby meeting offender, community, and employer needs.
• Conducting research on various reentry programs that may be suitable for implementation
• Determining the availability of funding
• Identification of housing needs and the assessment of the current level and quality of resources available.
• Mental health treatment and services.
• Proposed legislation, policies and practices that will facilitate the reentry of formerly incarcerated persons.
• The identification of service needs of those affected by criminal and addictive behavior related to substance abuse.
• The identification of resources currently available that can increase the capacity of organizations to provide services for formally incarcerated persons and their families.

Reentry Council Steering Committees identify services which may include:

1. Evidence Based Practices
2. Funding
3. Housing
4. Employment/Vocational Development
5. Mental Health
6. Substance Abuse
7. Policy and Law
8. Faith-based Support Systems
9. Community Support
10. Transitional Preparation
11. Health Care

Similar community collaborations or reintegration councils may also be structured in conjunction with the Community Corrections Departments to evaluate crminogenic risk factors. This group should work with community policing, prosecution, and court programs in order communicate the risk factors and assist in the reintegration process. This group can also develop into a *pre-sentence community sentencing review panel with* the goal to minimize the politics and increase substance associated with the punishment process. The judiciary will make the final sentencing decision but the recommendations provided by the sentencing review panel will provide the judiciary with a comprehensive understanding of the causes of the anti-social behavior, and will assist the judiciary and/or the jury in their sentencing decisions. The combination of the existing pre-sentence and reentry /post sentence report is also recommended. The Reintegration Council can also work in conjunction with a community transition program.

In 1999, the Indiana State Legislature passed a law known as the Community Transition Statute which may be found at (**http://www.in.gov/legislative/ic/code/title11/ar12/ch10.html**). This statute allows each county in the state to develop its own Community Transitions Program, to which inmates at the Department of Corrections may be released early to community supervision. It allows each county's judges to determine what level of supervision would be used. The statute excludes the following individuals from consideration for the early release program:

- Nonresidents of the State of Indiana
- Individuals with active warrants or detainers
- Individuals not serving a minimum two-year sentence

Allen County, Indiana supported state legislation because they mirrored national statistics that approximately 45 percent of offenders were returned to prison for technical violations or new charges within the first year after their release from prison. The percentage increased to nearly 67 percent after the three years following release. In 1999, Indiana State Legislature passed a law known as the Community Transitions Program. [1]

Allan County Community Corrections reports that after examining the above statistics, Allan County conceived the idea of a voluntary, 12-month "Reentry Court" program. This program is funded by reallocating existing resources at the state and county levels. The program supervises participants for the first four to six months of their release under electronic monitoring, while also providing *direct access to assistance with issues facing the returning offenders (i.e., reentry council resources).* The mission of the program is to significantly lower the rate of recidivism of returning offenders through gradually decreasing levels of supervision and enhanced delivery of services while maintaining public safety.

The Reentry Court is able to draw from a number of programs that offer activities designed to facilitate the reintegration of offenders into the community. In addition to the supervision discussed previously, the Court utilizes the following programs: GED classes and other educational programs through local post-secondary institutions, soft skill pre-employment training, cognitive skill development, sex offender intervention and treatment, violence intervention programs, crisis intervention, substance abuse programs, assistance with reinstatement of a Driver's License, and victim/offender conferencing. Additionally, Allen County Community Corrections has developed a 30-hour employment academy to better equip participants for reentering the workforce and to assess their motivation to obtain and maintain employment. The community mental health center also provides direct access to services and medications for mentally ill participants, and the Division of Family and Social Services provides expedited access to benefits for qualifying participants.

Faith-based organizations have been actively involved in the Reentry Court since its inception. The **Unity Christ Church** developed the "Unity of Love Family Reconnect Program" to help returning offenders successfully reintegrate into their families. They provide family dinner workshops where the participant and his/her family members share a meal with volunteers and staff members from the program. In addition to providing fellowship time with members of their own families, the program provides information on how to develop successful family relationships. The program also provides recreational time for the families that participate.

The faith-based community has also been instrumental in providing mentors for Reentry Court Program participants. Mentors are required to complete the training curriculum and are mentoring participants who have agreed to be part of the mentoring program. The coordinator of the mentoring program is involved in an ongoing process of recruiting, training, and overseeing additional mentors. Some faith-based organizations also assist returning offenders with housing. Five halfway houses in the city that are faith-based also have continued to provide housing and programming for offenders returning to the Reentry Court program.

Allan County Corrections further explained that since the statistics showed that 63 percent of the offenders returning to Allen County, Indiana, were returning to the southeast quadrant of the City of Fort Wayne, Phase I of Reentry Court Program focused the two-year pilot program in that area. If the program turned out to be successful, it would be expanded to the entire county. The first offenders were released to the program in June 2001. Phase I of the Reentry Court Program concluded on June 30, 2003. Preliminary evaluations of the program were favorable, and on July 1, 2003, the Reentry Court Program was expanded to parolees being released to the entire county. As of July 1, 2004 probation cases are included in Phase III of the program. Currently there are approximately 160 offenders under the supervision of the Reentry Court Program. For details of this program, please refer to the Allan County Web page: **http://www.allencountycorrections.com/services/reentry.shtml** (2006) [2]

Sociology Reference:

Justice: A concept referring to fairness and to the process of people getting what they deserve. In a legal sense, justice consists of treating everyone according to the law, of guaranteeing civil rights, and following prescribed procedures in a consistent manner.

Notes

1.   The Center on Juvenile and Criminal Justice reported that almost of 37,000 inmates entering the Texas prison system in 1998, more than two out of every three entered prison on a parole or probation violation. Of these, an estimated half were charged not with breaking the law by committing new crimes, but for committing technical violations, such as missing a meeting with a parole officer. A study released by the U.S. Department of Justice in June 2002, (Texas was included in the study), entitled *Recidivism of Prisoners Released in 1994* reported that within three years of release in 1994, 61.7 percent of offenders sentenced for violence were arrested for a new offense.

2.   The National Institute of Corrections will assist states in structuring their transition programs. The NIC model utilizes evidenced based practices in this process.

STEP 13-G

Institutional Corrections

While the care, custody, and control of inmates have been the primary missions of prisons and jails, these responsibilities must be expanded to include providing inmates with the tools and environment to make behavioral changes and reintegrate into the community.

The inmate management system at the Orange County Corrections Division in Florida uses a stair-stepped classification system that defines the parameters within which inmates must function and places them in control of their status and placement. Jail inmates are assigned to one of four housing categories, including booking, assessment center, special housing and maximum-security units, and programming. This continuum of care lets those offenders who choose to do so take responsibility and be held accountable for their lives. The way to ensure lasting change in an inmate's behavior is to establish *performance* measurements that can also be monitored in the community. All parts of the community and corrections system must work together to place the offender in the appropriate level of control to prohibit criminal activity (Allison 1993). It can be implied that that a stair –stepped classification system at the institutional level would function more efficiently if it were accompanied by structured sentencing guidelines.

Should one agent of the criminal justice system be responsible for a comprehensive sentencing plan? Miceli's (1994) sentencing model mistakenly assumes that one agent of the criminal justice system chooses both the length of the sentence and the length of the parole period, but in reality different agents with different mandates choose them independently. Agents with varying mandates have control over budgets, sentence length, rehabilitation opportunities, parole etc: therefore it is unlikely that a fragmented approach of this type will be efficient or function effectively within an organized inmate classification system. However, contrasting viewpoints suggest that *sentencing reform* should be more focused and systemically coordinated. These same experts have cited *three correctional policy issues that should be addressed in the decade ahead:* (1) whether sentencing policy should be linked to the management of correctional resources (i.e., available prison capacity); (2) whether concern for rehabilitation should be integrated in a sentencing model that emphasizes just deserts; and (3) whether parole boards should be retained and their role in a structured sentencing system. ("Sentencing Reform and Correctional Policy." From

Public Policy, Crime, and Criminal Justice, Second Edition, pp. 265-279 edited by Barry W. Hancock and Paul M. Sharp 2000: See NCJ-183970) NCJ 183964).

If you choose to work within the correctional policy issues delineated above and use sentencing guidelines, a proposal by Thomas Tabasz may be useful. Tabasz (1974) proposes a two-part sentencing scheme; also acknowledged as a *split sentence.* A split sentence authorizes punishment at the community and institutional levels. It is recommended to use this type of a sentencing scheme in the proposed Integrated Justice Model (IJM) in this text (Appendix C). IJM incorporates a multi-dimensional corrections strategy that includes a *combination* of the restraint, reform, rehabilitation and reintegration models but *does not suggest incarceration as a last resort.* In fact, incarceration may be used in the first phase of the sentence and community supervision in the second phase. The benefit of this model is its flexibility. It has the capacity to easily incorporate changes and adapt to the organizational environment when addressing the punishment process.

Tabasz suggests that the first part of the sentence may be used to target retribution. It would be determinate, independent of offender characteristics, of a short duration, and served in an institutional setting with no amenities. In the second phase, the offender would move on to a different environment to serve out the second, indeterminate state directed to the rehabilitation goal. Tabasz suggests that the condition of release would be some readily visible sign of achievement on the part of the offender, such as the attainment of an educational or vocational training goal. The literature suggests that a constitutional issue may exist with this model as it relates to the offender serving their "debt to society," identified in the first phase. However, the progressive rewards approach delineated in the second phase would be an improvement over the issues that arise from the existing crime control model, which lacks rehabilitation and reintegration programs and exacerbates crime and community safety issues.

The following study (Smith et al. 2006) summarizes the first national review of the recidivism and post-release employment effects of the Prison Industries Enhancement Certification Program (PIECP), which has been placing State prison inmates in private-sector jobs since 1979.

The study found that inmates who worked in open-market jobs in PIECP were significantly more successful in obtaining and remaining in post-release employment than those inmates who worked in traditional correctional industries (TI) or were involved in other than work (OTW) activities while in prison. TI releasees obtained postrelease employment quicker than OTW releasees. PIECP releasees earned significantly more than OTW releasees and were employed significantly more quarters after release than TI and OTW releasees.

PIECP releasees had slower and reduced recidivism measured by arrest, conviction, and incarceration than did TI and OTW releasees.

Given these findings, this report recommends increasing efforts to involve private businesses in the employment of inmates under the PIECP. PIECP programs may be "employer" model establishments, in which private-sector firms are often located inside correctional institutions, manage the PIECP inmate population, and produce goods for sale in open markets. The PIECP "customer" model may also be used. Under this model, departments of correction operate the PIECP production facilities, manage PIECP workers, and deliver products to private firms for sale in open markets. The PIECP may also be a "manpower" model, in which inmates are supervised by a private company but are considered to be employed by the department of correction.

This evaluation reviewed outcome records for 3 matched samples (PIECP, TI, and OTW inmates), each composed of approximately 2,200 inmates (a total of 6,464 inmates) released from 46 prisons across 5 PIECP States between 1996 and 2001.

In Texas, the Prison Industry Enhancement (PIE) Certification Program is a partnership between the Texas Department of Criminal Justice (TDCJ) and a private company, allowing the company to employ offenders who have volunteered to be a part of the program. The offenders are paid by the private company and deductions are taken from those wages to help pay for the offender's room and board, dependent support, and restitution, while a contribution is made to a crime victims fund.

The PIE Certification Program was created by Congress in 1979 to encourage states and units of local government to establish employment opportunities for offenders in realistic working environments, pay them wages, and enable them to acquire marketable skills to increase their potential for successful rehabilitation and meaningful employment upon release.

This year marks the 14th year of the PIE Certification Program in Texas. During these 14 years the program has evolved from a small program employing (11) offenders at one private facility, to a program that employed 458 offenders, at one private facility and three TDCJ units by the end of FY 05. The PIE program began operations under the aegis of the Parole Division in 1993. In an effort to expand the program, it was moved to Manufacturing and Logistics in 2000. During the past six years, the program has more than doubled the number of offenders employed and is on track to quadruple the amount of money that is repaid to the state in the form of room and board. [1]

Sociology Reference:

Justice: A concept referring to fairness and to the process of people getting what they deserve. In a legal sense, justice consists of treating everyone according to the law, of guaranteeing civil rights and following prescribed procedures in a consistent manner.

Works Cited

Allison, T.L., "Making Offenders More Accountable And Offering Opportunity For Change" *Corrections Today* Volume: 55 Issue: 6 (October 1993) Pages: 92-95 NCJ-145222 Pearson Education, Inc. Upper Saddle River, New Jersey, pp. 101.

Hancock, Barry W. and Paul M. Sharp (2000) Sentencing Reform and Correctional Policy (From *Public Policy, Crime, and Criminal Justice,* Second Edition, pp. 265-279. NCJ-183970) NCJ 183964).

Miceli, Thomas J. 1994. 'Prison and Parole: Minimizing the Cost of Non monetary Sanctions as Deterrents". *Research in Law and Economics* 16: 197-211.

Smith, Cindy J. et.al. 2006 "U.S. Department of Justice Correctional Industries Preparing Inmates for Reentry: Recidivism and Post-release Employment," *National Institute of Justice,* United States May 10, 2006

Tabasz, Thomas F. 1974. "Penology, Economics, and the Public: Toward an Agreement. *Policy Sciences* 5: 47-55.

Notes

1.   In 2007, there are approximately 150,000 Texas prison inmates and only approximately 1,000 inmates are utilizing the Prison Industry Enhancement Program or (0.6%).

STEP 13-H

Planning and the Punishment Process

As previously suggested, correctional policy must be removed from the political arena, so as to facilitate more rational and consistent policy development and implementation (Brownlee 1998). Punishments must be used that provide adequate retribution for offending behavior, together with reasonable levels of protection from further offending. Creative punishment strategies have been developed in an attempt to design a mode of constructive punishment that considers the needs and characteristics of the offender and his/her motivation. They make use of professional knowledge, such as psychology, which is useful in the sentencing process. They also accentuate the differences between the handling of both violent and nonviolent offenders with a sufficient punitive element that can satisfy the demand for justice and reduce recidivism (Henderson, J.H., 1982). The literature suggests that the lack of understanding of the concepts of punishment and how to plan and administer its fundamental principles, adversely impacts the offender, the institution, and the community. The literature also suggests that these inconsistencies may also be reasons for the ineffectiveness of rehabilitation programs and increased offender recidivism rates.

The basic concept of punishment is associated with deterrence theory. It would be difficult, if not impossible, to determine how many conformists would become deviants if they were not deterred by the fear of punishment (Toby 1964). However, deterrence theory suggests that you will refrain from deviance because of the fear of punishment (Ward 1994). There are two types of deterrence, general and specific. General deterrence affects the non-offending groups of our society because they are aware that other individuals have been punished. Specific deterrence deters persons that have been punished for a past deviant act. Ward explains that deterrence theorists identify three properties of punishment that should have an affect on deviance. The first property is certainty of punishment; the greater the perceived certainty of punishment, the less chance an individual will engage in a deviant act. The second property of punishment is severity. The greater the perceived severity of punishment, the less likely a person will engage in a deviant act. The third property of punishment is celerity, or swiftness. Deterrence theory suggests that if punishment is perceived to be immediate or swift, it should have a greater deterrent effect. David D. Perlmutter, senior associate for research at the Reilly Center for Media and Public Affairs at Louisiana State University, explains that "the next time your five year old pours molasses on the family cat, tell him that as a deterrent to future bad behavior you will take away his stereo upon his graduation from college. No punishment deters if it is unconnected to the crime in time and space" (Dallas Morning News Section 23A: Date N/A).

Policy Studies Professor Mark Kleiman explains that the deterrence factor of punishment is minimized because the severity factor of punishment takes precedence over certainty and celerity. [1] In other words, he emphasized: "don't let the price of crime go down." Certainty and celerity should be first, creating an order that is more conducive to deterrence. It can be implied that the proper management of punishment within a system that fits the punishment to the crime is essential when addressing equitable forms of justice. It can also be implied that the establishment of equal treatment will also enhance social control factors. Therefore, it should not be whether to punish but how. Punishment is based on the norms and living standards of society at large (Petersilia 1990). Petersilia suggests that with mitigating circumstances implied, this approach omits two important facts: serious offenders neither accept nor abide by these norms or they would not be criminals. Second, most people who qualify today for prison come from communities where living conditions fall far below standards than most Americans would realize (pp.454). If their values and standards are currently in contrast, their perceptions of punishment are not the same. In fact, most prisoners in today's prisons are no longer in isolation but the newly admitted inmate will probably find friends, if not family already there (pp.456).

The concept of punishment is more socially than individually based. A useful place to begin to describe this phenomenon is with Kant's explanation of deserved punishment (i.e., retribution) (Hirsch 1976). He based his concept of punishment on fairness. When someone infringes another's rights, the person gains an unfair advantage over others in society. The punishment for this act imposes a counterbalance disadvantage on the offender and restores balance (Hirsch 1976 pp.147). The literature suggests that the *fairness* concept can be applied to decisions made within the criminal justice system. It can be argued that if the social control agents are unjust regarding the administration of punishment (i.e., undeserved, unfair, unnecessary, or extreme) a "social crime" may be perceived by the offender, therefore the offender perceives society as having an unfair advantage. As a result of these actions, social retaliation could be committed by the offender, in the form of prejudice, hostility, resistance, a criminal act, and other acts of deviance in order to maintain the social equilibrium.

Understanding that the above viewpoint is purely speculation derived from the review of the literature, it was found that offenders who regarded punishment as a "deserved" misfortune for their own wrongdoing, were more *susceptible to rehabilitation* (Toby 1964). In fact, the way punishment is practiced in Western societies it is usually an obstacle to rehabilitation (Toby 1964 pp.58). It was also found that if the sentencing disposition of convicted offenders were more commensurate with the gravity of their crime, even if greater or less aus-terity would promote other goals, the likelihood for successful treatment strate-gies and reduced recidivism would follow (Hirsch 1976 pp.152). Therefore, based on this principle, it can be argued that understanding of the concepts of punishment may lead to social prerequisites for justice that may be more "solu-tions" based, whereas deterrence, incapacitation, and rehabilitation are more subsequent strategies for the "control" of crime.

It was found that a planned system of sentencing guidelines may be considered one of the solutions to finding *this fair and equitable* distribution of punishments (U.S. Department of Justice 1997). For example, in many states, commissions have plans in place addressing the integration of intermediate sanc-tions into sentencing guidelines and are devising systems of interchangeability between prison and non-prison sanctions (U.S. Department of Justice 1997 pp. 29-30). [2] The literature suggests that sentencing guidelines offer solutions to the problem of disparities found in the judicial sentencing process and may also assist in prisoner classification at the institutional level by providing *sentencing policy linked to the management of correctional resources.*). For example, sta-tistical comparisons of sentencing tendencies in various jurisdictions show that disparities are widespread. In the Detroit Recorder's Court, sentencing disposi-tions were sampled from ten judges over a twenty-month period. Findings re-vealed that one judge imposed prison terms upon as many as *90 percent* of the defendants he sentenced, while another judge ordered prison sentences on *35 percent* of similar cases (Inciardi, 1993). The literature suggests that the impact of these sentencing practices increases prison populations but the most signifi-cant finding is that when prisoners compare their sentences, and if the sentence is deemed unfair or they feel they are a victim of judicial prejudice, then hostil-ity, resistance to correctional treatment, and even a riot-prone environment can exist (Inciardi 1993 pp.452). [3]

The Office of Court Administration (OCA) reports that in 1993 the Texas Punishment Standards Commission and the Texas Criminal Justice Policy Council provided case-level information addressing incarceration rates and prison sentences in Texas. [4] This information explained that incarceration rates (number of people sent to prison per 100,000 in the population) varied widely by jurisdiction. Harris County sent 635 (per 100,000) to prison, Dallas County sent 465, and Bexar County sent 260. The data suggests that Texas prison sentencing may be disparate and since this study has not been replicated again since 1993 it needs further investigation.

A sentencing strategy that can effectively address these issues with the least amount of resistance is the development of statistical tables that reflect the aver-age sentences imposed by the judge within their local jurisdiction, broken down by the seriousness of the crime and the characteristics of the offender. This process will make it possible for a judge to know in advance of sentencing a case what his or her peers have done in similar circumstances, thus minimizing the possibility of judicial prejudice (pp. 454). This approach is considered a peer-based sentencing "recommendation" versus a sentencing guideline.

The National Center for State Courts (NCSC) Sentencing Project promotes ten sentencing policies to improve the effectiveness of sentencing outcomes, reduce recidivism, reduce over-reliance on incarceration, and promote community corrections and intermediate sanctions programs:

1)   Explicitly include risk and recidivism reduction as key objectives of effective state sentencing policy.
2)   Ensure that state sentencing policy allows sufficient flexibility for judges to implement risk reduction strategies.
3)   Promote the use of actuarial risk assessment instruments in assessing suitability of sentencing options.
4)   Create offender-based data and sentencing support systems that facilitate data-driven sentencing decisions.
5)   Develop effective community-based corrections programs that address the criminogenic needs of felony offenders.
6)   Develop community-based intermediate sanctions appropriate to the nature of committing offenses and offender risks.
7)   Provide judges and advocates with access to accurate and relevant sentencing data & information.
8)   Include a curriculum on Evidence Based Practices (EBP) in judicial education programs for sentencing judges.
9) Ensure effective collaboration among local criminal justice agencies to reduce barriers to risk reduction.
10)   Revise sentencing processes to support risk reduction strategies.

Currently there are sentencing commissions in 22 states, and a National Association of State Sentencing Commissions, supported by the Federal Sentencing Commission. Sentencing commission profiles are available as of 1997. Many of these strategies are beginning to take shape, for example, in Texas, through the efforts of the legislature, the Texas Department of Criminal Justice, the Community Assistance Division, and the Community Supervision and Corrections Departments. However, *the major missing pieces are #4 and #7, which concern the systematic collection and analysis of information about sentencing decisions.* **www.courts.state.tx.us/pubs/courtex/jan07.pdf.** Issues associated with the collection and analysis of information is also being addressed by the Texas Integrated Justice Information Systems Advisory Group (TIJIS). For more information on this group see the Web site at **www.tijis.org**.

Through an effective planning process, North Carolina and Ohio have adopted sentencing guidelines and have incorporated the use of intermediate sanctions that are interchangeable between prison and non-prison sanctions.

Pennsylvania and Massachusetts re-designed their sentencing guidelines utilizing the same strategy. (U.S. Department of Justice 1997).

The North Carolina model suggests that sentencing guidelines with the incorporation of intermediate sanctions can work. The North Carolina sentencing guidelines covers all felonies and misdemeanors with an attempt to increase use of prison sentences for violent crime. They reduced prison use for nonviolent crimes by using intermediate sanctions. In 1995, after the first full year of operation under this system, 81percent of violent felons received prison sentences, up 67 percent in 1993. Twenty-three percent of non-violent felons were sent to prison, down from 42 percent in 1993. For all imprisoned felons, the mean time to be served increased from 16 to 37 months (U.S. Department of Justice 1997). In this case, the literature suggests that sentencing guidelines provided to be the vehicle necessary for *"fitting the punishment to the crime."*

The Center on Juvenile and Criminal Justice (**www.cjcj.org**) found that Texas prison populations were disproportionate with non violent inmates. Contrary to the view that most of the people entering Texas prisons represent a threat to public safety, in 1998 the majority of prisoners in the Lone Star State were serving sentences for non-violent offenses. When the composition of the prison population was examined, most offenders were being incarcerated for low level crimes.[5]

- In 1998, the Texas Department of Criminal Justice reported that of its then 130,000 prisoners, 54.8 percent were being held for a non-violent crime. If these offense proportions held true for the 1999 BJS prison counts, there would be 89,428 inmates held for non-violent crimes in Texas. Just by itself, Texas' non-violent prison population represents the second largest state prison population in the country (next to that of California). Texas' non-violent prisoner population was larger than the entire incarcerated population of the United Kingdom (73,545), a country of 60 million people, and bigger than that of the prison system in New York, our 3rd largest state.
- Of the almost 37,000 inmates entering the Texas prison system in 1998, more than *two out of every three entered prison on a parole or probation violation.* Of these, an estimated half were charged not with breaking the law by committing new crimes, but for committing technical violations, such as missing a meeting with a parole officer
- Twenty one percent (21 percent) of the people in Texas prisons are there for drug related charges. While a large number on its own, the 21 percent figure understates the role drug incarceration policies have played in driving up the prison population totals, as it does not include people serving time for drug related crimes such as theft or burglary. Eighty-five percent of the prison population has a history of drug or alcohol abuse.

This literature suggests that improved criminal justice *planning* may be a key component to "fighting crime" by developing an improved sentencing process that requires a more balanced use of community corrections, intermediate sanctions and prison; and one that when used properly will establish longer prison terms for serious and habitual criminals. The literature further suggests that an improved sentencing process will also establish a rational and consistent sentencing standard, which will *reduce sentencing disparities* and ensure that sanctions following convictions are proportional to the severity of the offense. Because the capacities of state and local correctional facilities are limited, use of *incarcerative sanctions should be restricted to those convicted of more serious offenses or those who have longer criminal histories.*[6]To ensure such usage of resources, sanctions used in sentencing convicted felons should be the least restrictive necessary to achieve the purposes of the sentence. Furthermore, it was inferred that these changes could lead to resolution of punishment issues deemed "inequitable," by preventing the inconsistencies found when attempting to manage punishment and improve the offender reintegration process.

Sociology Reference:

Social Control: A concept that refers to the ways in which people's thoughts, feelings, appearance, and behavior are regulated in social systems. Control may be exerted through various forms of coercion such as the authority of the criminal justice system. Coercion, however, is generally ineffective as the sole means of social control. Far more important is socialization through which people come to identify with the social system and its values and norms and acquire a stake in maintaining these as well as their sense of belonging to the system. Fear of ridicule or exclusion is a powerful inducement to conform as well as the risk of being shamed.

Justice: A concept referring to fairness and to the process of people getting what they deserve. In a legal sense, justice consists of treating everyone according to the law, of guaranteeing civil rights, and following prescribed procedures in a consistent manner.

Works Cited

Brownlee, I. 1998, Restorative justice in community corrections. *Corrections Today*, 58 52-155.

Perlmutter, David, "Killings strengthen case for death penalty" *Dallas Morning News*, Sec. 23-A. Date unavailable.

Henderson, J.H. 1982 Interface between law enforcement and psychology: a case study of creative punishment and alternatives to incarceration". *Police Journal*, 55(3): 285-289.

Hirsch, Andrew Von. 1976 *"Doing Justice: The Choice of Punishments"* *pp.161-165 (New York:Hill & Wang* (reprint, *Criminal Justice Vol.3 (Sage Publications, 1996): 147, 152.*

Inciardi, J.A. 1993 Criminal Justice, 4th ed. pp. 451-455. San Diego, CA: Harcourt Brace College Publishers.

Petersilia, J. 1990 "When Probation Becomes More Dreaded Than Prison", *Federal Probation,* Vol. 54, No. 1, 23-27 (reprint, *The Dilemmas of Corrections* 3rd ed. pp. 454-455.Waveland Press, Inc., 1995).

Toby, J. 1964 "Is Punishment Necessary?" *Journal of Criminal Law, Criminology, and Police Science,* 55, 58 332-337 (reprint, *Criminal Justice* Vol. 3 (Sage Publications 1996), 155.

U.S. Department of Justice 1997 Intermediate Sanctions in Sentencing Guidelines, OJP, May Issue NCJ 165043: pp. xii, 29-30

Ward, David A., Carter, Timothy J. and Perrin, Robin D., *Social Deviance,* 1994 pp. 37 Needham Heights, MA 02194 Simon and Schuster, Inc.

Notes

1. C-Span, Presentation Sponsored by the National Institute of Justice (NIJ) (December 4, 1998)
2. Currently there are sentencing commissions in 22 states within the U.S.
3. The Minnesota Sentencing Guidelines suggest that the purpose of sentencing guidelines is to establish rational and consistent sentencing standards, which reduce sentencing disparity and ensure that sanctions following conviction for a felony are proportional to the severity of the crime and criminal history. Because the capacities of state and local correctional facilities are finite, the use of incarcerative sanctions should be limited to those convicted of more serious offenses or those who have longer criminal histories.
4. Court Tex, *Texas Judicial Branch News:* Special Edition: State Sentencing Policy, January, 2007.
5. The authors of this report were Dana Kaplan, Vincent Schiraldi, and Jason Ziedenberg of the Justice Policy Institute. This report was funded by a grant from the Open Society Institute's Center on Crime, Communities, and Culture.
6. Incarceration can work to control and deter crime if administered properly. Studies indicate that a small percentage of offenders commit over half of all violent crimes. If these violent offenders were imprisoned, the nation would experience a significant drop in violent crime. However, is those cases where the majority of convicted criminals are not violent, when sentenced to prison it reduces prison space and negates this approach.

STEP 14-15

ACCOMPLISHMENT OF GOALS AND OB-JECTIVES ARE THE PRIMARY MISSION FOR THE ORGANIZATION

In this section, managing for results is explained and linked to organizational performance measures. It discusses the need to establish a performance measurement process, and the use and reporting of performance measures in order for management, elected officials, and the public, to assess the degree of success the organization has in accomplishing its mission, goals, and objectives. In order to effectively accomplish the organizational goals and objectives, management and leadership characteristics are paramount.

The "Managing for Results" concept is a good example of how you can effectively incorporate performance measures into the mission and goals of the organization. The Government Accounting Standards Board (GASB), sponsored by the Alfred P. Sloan Foundation, defines Managing for Results by delineating performance measures as an important tool for understanding government performance, but clarifies that without a *process* for using this information, it is only of limited value. One such process that is receiving increased interest in government, as well as in the not-for-profit and the private sector, is called *Managing for Results (MFR)*. The "managing for results" process is a comprehensive approach to aiding public policy and administrative organizations focusing on their missions, goals, and objectives. It establishes the accomplishment of those goals and objectives as the primary endeavor for the organization, and provides a systematic method for carrying out that endeavor. It requires the (1) establishment of *performance measures*, (2) use, and (3) reporting of those measures so that management, elected officials and the public can assess the degree of success the organization has in accomplishing its mission, goals, and objectives.

The GASB delineates seven basic steps for the MFR process. On paper they are presented as discrete and separate; however, they are in fact interwoven and should feed back, forth, and across.

1. Planning for results (strategic planning)
2. Program (activity) planning

3. Developing meaningful performance measures
4. Budgeting for results
5. Managing work processes and collecting data
6. Evaluating and responding to results
7. Reporting results

The GASB explains that there is no one "right" way in implementing a Managing for Results program. Every municipality, state, organization, or department has many different variables of complexity and size and as a result, the goals, objectives, and priorities will be different for each one. The seven steps mentioned above are a guideline to consider when implementing a Managing for Results program.

For example, The Department of Health and Mental Hygiene for the State of Maryland implemented Managing for Results (MFR) in order to meet the needs of Maryland's customers and stakeholders more effectively and efficiently. It was deemed a future-oriented strategic process that emphasizes achieving results that are both meaningful and measurable. Managing for Results is prepared by the Department of Health and Mental Hygiene (DHMH) as part of the *operating budget* and is updated annually. Departmental goals are outlined in the Departmental Summary, and each program has identified goals and objectives that are outcome-oriented and address the mission of the unit. The MFR plans reflect strategic planning decisions in DHMH and the individual programs. Managing for Results plans include the following elements: Program Description, Mission Statement, Vision Statement, Key Goals and Objectives, and Performance Measures. The states of Florida, Illinois, Iowa, Louisiana, Maine, Michigan, Minnesota, New Mexico, Oklahoma, Texas and Oregon have also implemented various components of the MFR process.

Maricopa County, Arizona has implemented a MFR process and has incorporated it into their budget process in order to establish greater coordination of performance management. Maricopa leveraged a countywide strategic planning process, a common budget process, and countywide performance reporting. All departments are required to participate in the strategic planning process and priorities and goals are established with shared responsibilities among *elected, judicial, and appointed departments*. All departments must follow the same format for budget submittals, performance measures are required for all programs, and any additional funding must be *tied to strategic goals* and performance measures. Measured results are entered into the MFR data base and progress in achieving departmental strategic goals is addressed quarterly.

In order to effectively accomplish the organizational goals and objectives, management and leadership characteristics are essential. Leaders should be concerned for their people, but they also must have concern for production. The issue is how much attention should be provided to one or the other. The model below entitled the *Managerial Grid,* is an example of a   management strategy that identifies the differences between leadership traits. This strategy was introduced by Blake and Mouton in the early 1960s. The grid delineates individual leadership characteristics, on a continuum with low concern for people and production as the worst trait and high concern for people and production the best trait.

Figure 3: A rendition of the original Blake and Mouton *Managerial Grid:* The Managerial Grid Model (1964) is a behavioral leadership model developed by Robert Blake and Jane Mouton. The below model identifies different leadership styles based on the concern for people and the concern for production and can be found at **www.changingminds.org**

Concern for People	High	Country Club management		Team management
	Medium		Middle of the road management	
	Low	Impoverished management		Authority-compliance
The *Managerial Grid* (Defined by Blake and Mouton -1964)		*Low*	*Medium*	*High*
		Concern for Production (Task)		

The aforementioned leadership characteristics are described as follows:

1.   Impoverished management

Minimum effort to get the work done. A basically lazy approach that avoids as much work as possible.

2.   Authority-compliance

Strong focus on task, but with little concern for people; Focus on efficiency, including the elimination of people wherever possible.

3.   Country Club management

Care and concern for the people, with a comfortable and friendly environment and collegial style. But a low focus on task may give questionable results.

4.   Middle of the road management

A weak balance of focus on both people and the work. Doing enough to get things done, but not pushing the boundaries of what may be possible.

5.   Team management

Firing on all cylinders: people are committed to task and leader is committed to people (as well as task). For additional information on the *Managerial Grid* refer to the following Web site.
(**http://changingminds.org/disciplines/leadership/styles/managerial_grid.htm**)

The significant difference between managers and leaders is the way they motivate and influence the people who work or follow them to meet organization goals, and this sets the tone for most other aspects of what they do. Many individuals are both managers and leaders. However, it will take a leader to convince the employee to follow them down a difficult path, especially if they are attempting to change the direction of the organization, and following is always a voluntary activity. For additional information on the differences between managers and leaders, refer to the following Web site: **http://www.randomhouse.co.uk/features/leader/leader.html**

Figure 4: An overview of the original model developed by Warren Bennis 1989: *On Becoming a Leader.* Additional information on this topic can be found at **http://www.randomhouse.co.uk/features/leader/leader.html**

Managers	Leaders
Administer and copy	Innovation and originality
Maintain	Develop
Focus on Systems and Structure	Focus on People

Accomplishment of Goals and Objectives are the Primary Mission for the Organization

Rely on control	Inspire Trust
Short-Range View	Long-Range View
Ask How and When	Ask What and Why
Accept the Status Quo	Challenge the Status Quo
Do Things Right	Do The Right Things

Sociology Reference:

Leadership: Leadership is the ability to influence what goes on in a social system. In most cases, leadership is based on some form of legitimate authority associated with a social status, such as a manager or president.

Works Cited

Bennis, W. G. 1989. *On becoming a leader*. New York: Addison-Wesley Publishers.

Blake, Robert R. and Jane S. Mouton, 1964: *The Managerial Grid* Houston, Texas: Gulf Publishing.

STEP 16

UTILIZE THE AVAILABLE TECHNOLOGY

Utilize the available technology that will allow you to effectively analyze and share information. Most information systems operated by criminal justice agencies are discrete, and are usually incapable of linking and exchanging information effectively. Although improvements have been made, many aspects of the criminal justice information systems remain constrained by a lack of interoperability.

Technology

Technological deficiencies are found in within the principal categories of the criminal justice system: community, police, prosecution, courts, and corrections. There are also interoperability issues associated with the administrative functions of the criminal justice system, such as the inability to rely on information systems to support critical decision-making needs. Policymakers lack access to reliable data and statistics with which to measure the effectiveness of laws, policies, and programs.

For example:

• Crime victims need timely and reliable information about criminal cases and the custody status of offenders in order to be notified immediately upon a change in the inmate's status, such as a release, escape, or court appearance.

• The officer on the street who makes a traffic stop has immediate access to critical information about the driver and the vehicle. He knows within seconds whether the driver's license is current, whether the driver is wanted, or the vehicle stolen. However, as times have changed, the officer needs more information. For example, as revealed through crime analysis and intelligence and information sharing, is the driver an immediate threat to peace officers, or is the driver a terrorist?

- Prosecutors need complete and accurate information about not only the current case details, but also the defendant's previous background and criminal history in order to make accurate decisions about charging the subject.

- Judges hearing first appearances for arrested persons need to have a correct identification of the offender and comprehensive and accurate data on the subject's background and criminal history to make decisions concerning bail, pre-trial release, and *sentencing*.

- Prison and jail administrators need comprehensive and accurate information to properly segregate institutions, in order to manage and control inmate populations.

- Parole officers need comprehensive and accurate information on individuals released from prison in order to provide an efficient case management process, to manage and reintegrate the ex-offender into society.

- Policy makers need access to comprehensive data to measure the effectiveness of the criminal justice system.

Criminal justice entities have long recognized the urgency of developing a comprehensive strategy for the integration of cross-jurisdictional justice information systems. However, the concept of an "integrated justice information system" means different things to different people in different contexts, and it is important to clarify these perceptions and consolidate the strategies. In order to achieve this goal, the Texas Integrated Justice Information Systems (TIJIS) Steering Committee (**www.tijis.org**), a statewide technological advisory group, was established to assist in the coordination of statewide integrated justice information systems. This group is currently developing a statewide criminal justice reference model (i.e., blueprint) that addresses the above issues by identifying key data flows among producers and consumers of criminal justice data. Through the development of this model, representatives of the criminal justice system will have access to reliable data and statistics with which to measure the effectiveness of laws, policies, and programs. The Texas Office of Court Administration is encouraged by these efforts, because it anticipates that these efforts will lead to the establishment of improved *sentencing practices* by the creation of offender-based data and sentencing support systems that will facilitate data-driven sentencing decisions and provide judges and advocates with access to accurate and relevant sentencing data and information. This work is ongoing between the Office of Court Administration, with the guidance and encouragement of the Judicial Committee on Information Technology, and the members of the Texas Integrated Justice Information Systems Steering Committee. The Texas Department of Public Safety, currently developing the IJIS criminal justice reference model, is equally enthusiastic about these efforts because they believe that through the development of this reference model law enforcement agencies will be able to access and share reliable information relating to crime and *homeland security* issues as well as measure their overall effectiveness.

It is hoped that the use of this guide will provide you with the steps necessary to effectively coordinate and/or plan the criminal justice process within your current or future organization. Through effective planning, along with improved management practices and leadership within the criminal justice organization, a common purpose will be established resulting in a more efficient system of justice. These improvements will minimize systemic fragmentation and improve the effective administration of justice.   Finally, improved levels of collaboration and cooperation with the community, law enforcement, prosecution, the judiciary and corrections will result in what has been deemed the "measure of success" for the criminal justice system: reduced recidivism rates and community safety.

Sociology Concepts:

Technological Determinism: A view that social conditions and the characteristics of social systems are determined by technology and technological changes. It would view the Industrial Revolution or the introduction of computer technology as primary engines driving *social change* and shaping social relationships and institutions.

STEP 17

DESIGN A COMMUNITY BASED JUSTICE MODEL AND INCORPORATE INTO THE INTE-GRATED JUSTICE MODEL

The Community Justice Model

The below diagram is an illustration of a community justice model. The four traditional goals of sentencing remain (i.e., incapacitation, deterrence, punishment, and rehabilitation) but are considered in the context of reintegration. Note: Step 13, 13 A-H describes the programmatic strategy as it relates to community justice; the points addressed in Appendix D may be used as the checklist.

Figure 5: Community Justice Model

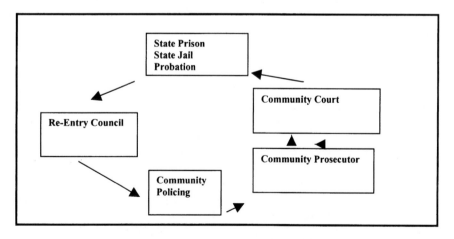

Source: Tarrant County Administrator's Office, Fort Worth, Texas (2007).

The first step when implementing a community justice model is to gauge the acceptance of the community justice strategy. A survey should be directed to city, county and state political leaders, law enforcement agencies, county district attorney's office, state probation departments, and local and state corrections agencies. The survey should address but is not limited to the following categories:

- Principles of Community Justice
- Traditional versus Contemporary Criminal Justice Practices
- Reentry Councils
- Punishment and Sentencing Practices
- Reintegration
- Evidence Based Practices
- Organizational Goals and Objectives
- Planning and Coordination
- Recidivism
- Technology
- Judicial and Court Practices

After the evaluation is finalized it is suggested to meet with each department and provide the results of the survey. The survey is considered one of the key components for successful program development. After the survey results have been communicated and the community justice strategy has been accepted there are four key areas that are necessary to address:

1. **Outline of Concept:** A succinct overview of the proposed community justice strategy that addresses the problem, supporting statistics, general review of existing resources, goal, target population, objectives, outputs, outcomes, efficiency measures, governance, and implementation. This document lays the foundation for the development of a community justice strategic plan.

2. **Project Charter:** A charter serves as the governing instrument for the development and *coordination of the reentry council.* The charter defines the project scope, management structure and the roles and responsibilities of its membership. It minimizes the risk that the project will be derailed as a result of error, misunderstanding or miscommunication.

3. **Position Paper:** A reentry council position paper establishes an *apolitical* position on the topic of reintegration.

4. **Program Development:** Hire a program coordinator and finalize the community justice strategic plan.

5. **Integration and Verification:** Incorporate the Community Justice Model and the Integrated Justice Model (Appendix C and Figure 7).

OVERVIEW OF
ORIGINAL RESEARCH
State Criminal Justice Systems within the U.S. and the Offender
Reintegration Process (Smith, L.J. 2003)

Methodology

Criminal justice planners were selected to provide additional support to this study because most of the planning literature reviewed was theoretical and was limited to resources that addressed collaborative planning. The National Association of Criminal Justice Planners (NACJP) and representatives from state criminal justice planning agencies across the United States were selected and provided a survey instrument. It should also be noted that there were only 27 criminal justice planners listed in 27 different states throughout the United States. Therefore, it can be speculated that there are a deficient number of criminal justice planners across the United States, that they are not participating in the planning association, or that they exist and are not active organizations.

Through the qualification of data collected from various professional journals, observational notes as a participant, review of public documents, examination of video tapes, text books, and Internet resources the planning and systemic functions of State criminal justice systems are examined. The planning and systemic functions were compared by conducting a content analysis of the systemic and planning processes of criminal justice systems. The analysis included the review of information collected The planning processes examined were long and short-term goals of the criminal justice system and cohesive and non-cohesive planning. The systemic functions examined were the criminal justice system's strategies of police enforcement and investigation, prosecution policy, judicial court administration and process, and the management of correctional institutions. The impact of these factors were weighed against the offender reintegration process and community safety.

The perceptions of criminal justice planners addressing the same categories were also measured by conducting a one-shot case study that evaluated the opinions of criminal justice planners currently practicing within the U.S. criminal justice system. The survey was divided into two sections and was comprised of 14 questions. The first section consisted of 10 questions that addressed the systemic functions of the criminal justice system and how these processes affected the offender reintegration process and community safety. The second section consisted of 4 questions addressing criminal justice planning processes. A frequency distribution was processed that measured the perceptions of criminal justice planners regarding the planning and systematic processes of the criminal justice system in their state, and its impact on the offender reintegration process and community safety.

Fifty surveys were mailed to each state within the United States. The first set of surveys were mailed directly to known criminal justice planners that are listed as current members of the National Association of Criminal Justice Planners in 27 different States. These states were Colorado, Kentucky, Louisiana, New York, Florida, Tennessee, Arizona, Ohio, Maryland, Texas, Minnesota, Michigan, Pennsylvania, Nevada, Oregon, South Carolina, Alabama, Hawaii, Washington D.C., Iowa, New Mexico, California, Washington, Wisconsin, Virginia, Nebraska, and Illinois. The remaining surveys were mailed to the other remaining 23 states. It was not known whether these states had criminal justice planners; therefore, the survey was forwarded to the Governor's Office with instructions requesting that a criminal justice professional complete the survey.

Findings

Criminal justice planners from 15 states responded to the survey, which resulted in a 30 percent response rate. The meager response rate may be indicative of the lack of governmental organizations addressing criminal justice planning, which supports this study's hypothesis. For the purpose of clarification, the study's hypothesis is repeated in this section.

Hypothesis: This study reviews the current state of academic literature as it pertains to the premise that United States criminal justice systems are fragmented and are not performing at functional levels. Furthermore, this study attempts to qualify that most state criminal justice experts support this premise. Finally, the study seeks to affirm that as the organization's environmental conditions (e.g., legal, political, economic, and cultural) continue to influence the mission of the criminal justice system, improved planning efforts will result in strategies that can improve contemporary justice models and prompt the system to perform more efficiently.

It should be noted that there were only 27 criminal justice planners listed as members of the National Association of Criminal Justice Planners *representing 27 different states*. Therefore, considering that only 11 of the 27 NACJP members responded (41 percent response rate) and 5 of the 23 non-NACJP planners responded (32 percent response rate), the 16 states that responded represent a 59 percent response rate from *known planners* across the United States. The non-NACJP states that responded to the survey were Rhode Island, Wyoming, North Carolina, Massachusetts, and Mississippi.

When asked about the planning and management processes of their state's criminal justice system, the majority (24 percent) of the respondents indicated that the criminal justice system in their state was not functioning effectively; 16 percent verified that there was no cohesive planning process; 18 percent indicated that their criminal justice system was not unified and structured on mission, goals and strategic planning; and 18 percent believed that their criminal justice system was fragmented and lacked a system-wide agreement of mission, goals and strategic planning.

When asked questions regarding the systemic processes of the criminal justice system in their state as it relates to the offender reintegration process, the majority of the respondents (22 percent) indicated that law enforcement did not contribute to a successful reintegration process. The majority (24 percent) believed that prosecutors failed to address reintegration, (14 percent) of the judiciary and corrections neglected the reintegration process, and the majority (24 percent) failed to have a pre-adjudication offender reintegration plan in place.

It was found that 14 percent believed that judicial sentencing practices contributed to a successful reintegration process; 16 percent favored probation departments programs; 14 percent believed that management of correctional facilities led to successful reintegration; 22 percent believed that incarceration work programs contributed to offender success; 18 percent favored parole's efforts, and 14 percent believed that community safety was not in jeopardy.

Conclusion

The literature review and findings supported the hypothesis that changes in the organizational environment, led primarily by the development of the crime control model, inordinately fragmented the systemic functions of U.S. criminal justice systems and adversely impacted the total system outcomes. Although certain levels of fragmentation were expected to be found, the criminal justice planning process, or a lack thereof, was found to be the central problem. A new and more integrated justice model was also recommended that required higher levels of coordination and planning.

Appendix B

Jail Population –Prediction and Evaluation Variables

1. Size and distribution of population, location and size of urban areas, geographical size, crime rate, social and cultural norms, and the political and economic situation.

2. Evaluate the urban population variable. This variable is the number of individuals who live in the urban areas.

3. Evaluate the density of the population.

4. The frequency of crime (i.e., rate of crime per 100,000 inhabitants for a specific year compared to the UCR Crime report.

5. The unemployment rate.

6. Community demographics. The crime prone age group accounts for 30-35 percent of Part 1 UCR Index Crime.

7. Jail and prison populations vary based on climate, economic position, geographical area and size and density of the community. Large urban areas primarily in the south have higher rates of violence.

8. Total of reported crimes, arrests, cases filed, court filings (felonies and misdemeanors) categorized by demographic groups (i.e., gender, race and age groups) and compared to the percent of jail population. The highest percentages are normally found in violent and general arrests but the leading indicator is the demographic data within these parameters.

9. Evaluate the frequency of crime (i.e., rate of crime per 100,000 inhabitants for a specific year.

10. Calculate the average daily jail population.

11. Identify the seasonal highs and lows.

12. Calculate the hours an inmate is in custody and calculate a percent of these hours.

13. Calculate the average days the inmate has served.

14. Evaluate criminal classification of inmates (i.e., the percent of Felons, Misdemeanors, Parole violators etc.).

15. Evaluation of Pretrial Release operations.

16. Assess system issues associated with the arrest to filing of a court case.

17. The development of a criminal court case flow processes and docket management systems.

18. The records management process related to the judgment, sentencing and indictment process.

19. State parole revocations.

20. State prisoner transfer requirements.

21. The evaluation of existing programs that have a positive impact on jail population.

Integrated Justice Model

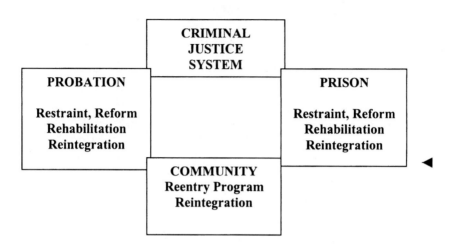

The Integrated Justice System Model (IJM) is a *combination* of the restraint, reform, rehabilitation and reintegration correctional models. IJM incorporates a multi-dimensional sentencing scheme that authorizes punishment to begin at any level of the system administered through one sentence. Chronic offending is considered long-term and in many cases interminable. The reform, rehabilitation and reintegration processes begin inside the institution and completed with the support of a community reentry program. Community justice strategies are also included and begin at the time of arrest and continue throughout the criminal justice process. The following two sentencing schemes are similar:

Michael Howard (1993), former Home Secretary of the United Kingdom, proposed a hybrid determinate/indeterminate sentencing scheme similar to "three strikes and you're out" strategies. Under this scheme, *repeat violent offenders* would automatically receive life sentences with the option of parole. The trail judge would set a minimum period intended to satisfy the need for retribution and deterrence. Once that period is served, authorities would determine if the inmate is released. Upon release the offender would be subject to recall the rest of their lives. Thomas Tabasz (1974) proposed a two-part penalty scheme. The first part of the sentence was determinate and targeted retribution. The offender would then pass on to a different environment to serve out the indeterminate phase directed towards the goal of rehabilitation.

Works Cited

Howard, Michael. 1996. In Defense of Prisons. *The Economist* (22 June): 56-57.

Tabasz, Thomas F. 1974. Penology, Economics, and the Public: Toward an Agreement. *Policy Sciences* 5:47-55

Community Justice Model
Checklist

1. ___Incorporate a community justice strategy that targets high-impact locations where there is a concentration of crime and criminal justice activities, in order to develop special localized community safety strategies

2. ___Incorporate an integrated justice strategy that includes a multi-dimensional sentencing scheme that allows punishment to begin at any level of institutional or community corrections administered through one sentence

3. ___Establish an ex-offender reentry council

4. ___Establish a reentry program and hire a coordinator

5. ___Develop local strategies that work to strengthen the capacity of your community

6. ___Develop partnerships with residents, businesses, and other social services to better coordinate the way public safety problems are addressed

7. ___Interact with the community to modify police and community activities to various problems residents perceive to be undermining their quality of life

8. ___Encourage the courts to become more familiar with the various community public-safety issues

9. ___Consider reintegration as an additional sentencing goal

10. ___Address the development of a reintegration plan before the sentencing phase of a trial

11. ___Address the need for correctional agency directors to have more input in the politics and policy development that determines the direction of correctional agencies

12. ___Consider the needs and characteristics of the individual offender and his/her motivation when administering punishment and treatment in order to provide protection from further offending

13. ___Prisons and jails should be expanded to include providing inmates with the tools and environment necessary to make behavioral changes in order to successfully reintegrate into the community

14. ___Have a management strategy available that establishes a perform-ance measurement process in order for management, elected officials and the public to assess the degree of success the organization has in accomplishing its mission, goals, and objectives

15. ___Have a strategy in place that considers a comprehensive approach to criminal justice planning that requires a cohesive planning process that includes community advocates, prevention organizations, state and local governments, political representatives and educational institutions

16. ___Recidivism rates are considered measures of how well the criminal justice system functions within a community

17. ___A jail population projection model is available that provides cycli-cal projections

18. [a7]___Criminal justice entities have a comprehensive strategy for an integrated justice information system that will improve cross jurisdic-tional justice information sharing and assist criminal justice officials with research and planning.

19. ___Consider a major change in leadership and managerial characteris-tics in order to assure the success of a community justice program

20. ___Reentry courts must be established and utilized to help reduce re-cidivism and improve public safety through increased use of judicial oversight

21. ___Community court programs must be established that focus on qual-ity-of-life offenses such as drug possession, shoplifting, vandalism, and prostitution.

22. ___Community-based prosecution programs must established that in-volve long-term, proactive partnerships among the prosecutor's office, law enforcement, the community

23. ___Community corrections must be committed to providing services through an evidence-based practice approach which is structured to meet the crminogenic needs of individual offenders through empirically based "what works" research in order to assist in the rehabilitation and reintegration process

24. ___Police must consider redefining their mission with a focus on be-coming more community-based and minimizing the reliance on tradi-tional law enforcement practices